CAREERS IN PRIVATE SECURITY

CAREERS IN PRIVATE SECURITY

How to Get Started, How to Get Ahead

Leigh Wade

Paladin Press • Boulder, Colorado

Careers in Private Security: How to Get Started, How to Get Ahead
by Leigh Wade

Copyright © 2002 by Leigh Wade

ISBN 1-58160-309-6
Printed in the United States of America

Published by Paladin Press, a division of
Paladin Enterprises, Inc.
Gunbarrel Tech Center
7077 Winchester Circle
Boulder, Colorado 80301 USA
+1.303.443.7250

Direct inquiries and/or orders to the above address.

PALADIN, PALADIN PRESS, and the "horse head" design
are trademarks belonging to Paladin Enterprises and
registered in United States Patent and Trademark Office.

Visit our Web site at www.paladin-press.com

Contents

Introduction

T his book has been written to assist people who want to get into the huge and growing field of private security. It is not a nuts-and-bolts manual on how to perform security functions, but should be used as a map of the industry to find out where you fit in and to give you some ideas about where you might like to go next. Hopefully, it will save both you and your prospective employer a lot of time and trouble, not only when you are just getting started but as you progress though your career.

The private security industry includes everything from one-man operations all the way up through gigantic multinational corporations that earn billions of dollars a year and employ hundreds of thousands of people. Although I say this book will help you find your place in the industry, I'm actually only talking about the lower,

1

operational end of the spectrum, or jobs you might find at a security company in a good-sized city. Once you get further up the corporate food chain, the importance of knowing security functions takes a back seat to the importance of knowing basic business procedures. If you already have business experience and a business degree, you don't need any advice from me.

One thing I need to mention right away, though, and something that needs to be emphasized: This book is about *private security*. This means I am talking about security services that are sold to buyers—in other words, business. The main purpose of any business is to make money for the owners and investors, not to provide the best possible service at any price as it so often is with government and military security agencies and departments.

Much of what you will read in this book comes from my own hard-earned experience. I first became interested in private security work 30 years ago, right after I got out of the U.S. Army the first time. I'd joined the army right out of high school and spent the next 10 years in Special Forces units fighting the Vietnam War, so I was pretty naive about the ways of civilian life and civilian jobs when I first reentered the job market. Let me tell you a little story about my first private security job.

After being discharged, I moved to Houston, Texas, and spent two or three months goofing off. When my savings were about gone I decided it was time to get a job. Police and security work appealed to me not only because it sounded like it might be exciting, but also because it was one of the few areas of civilian employment that sounded vaguely like what I had been doing in the army. I applied for several local and federal law enforcement jobs, and while I waited for results on those applications I took a look at the help wanted section in the newspaper. As they are today, the want ads were full of security jobs. I picked the company with the biggest ad, stuck my DD 214 (the document that identifies a veteran's condition of discharge—honorable or otherwise) in an envelope, and drove down to apply for work.

The company was national and one of the largest in the country. It had once been known primarily as a detective agency, and in fact still used the words "detective agency" in its company name. As I drove to their offices I had fantasies of myself wearing a trench coat and snap-brim hat, and carrying my trusty rod in a shoulder rig. As I said, I was pretty naive when I first got out of the army.

I parked my car, found the sign on the door that said "Employment Applications Here," and went on in. A young, bored, gum-chewing receptionist greeted me, handed me a 10-page application to fill out, and pointed to a chair and table. There were a couple of other men at the table already at work on their applications, one of them muttering and cursing under his breath.

The application was very detailed, I soon discovered, and it demanded I list every place I'd ever lived in my life and every employment and period of unemployment I'd had. In the army, I had been granted a top secret cryptographic security clearance that had necessitated a full background investigation, but the paperwork required for that clearance was nothing at all as detailed as the form these civilians had just handed me.

The other two guys at the table with me were evidently friends and had come in to apply together. They didn't smell very good, had long, greasy hair, and looked a lot like hippies to me. As I worked on my application, they finished theirs, and soon one of them was called in the inner sanctum for an interview. He was back out in about two minutes. He signaled with a nod of the head to his buddy and they both left together. Once outside the glass entrance door, the guy who had just been interviewed spun around, flipped the bird, and screamed, "Screw you bastards!" I presumed they hadn't gotten the job.

I finally finished my job application, turned it in to the receptionist who accepted it with a sneer, and after a short wait was called in to meet the personnel manager. He was a middle-aged guy in business attire, and he sat behind a desk cluttered with paperwork and overflowing ashtrays. He picked up the job application I had agonized over for almost an hour, merely glanced at it, and tossed in on a large pile of other applications. My DD 214 interested him more, however, and he took more time looking at it.

"So," he said, "just got out, huh?"

"Yessir," I promptly answered, trying not to sit at attention.

"Just back from Vietnam I see," he continued. "I was in World War II and the Korean thing."

"Yessir, yessir," I replied again.

"Ummm, see you carried a top secret clearance . . ."

"Yessir."

He fired up another Camel, leaned back in his chair and blew smoke out his nose. "So when can you start work?" he asked.

"Well," I said, "I guess I can start right away. I'm not working anyplace else."

"OK, great," he said, "let me turn you over to our supply person and fix you up with a uniform and get your fingerprints, then come back here when you get done and I'll have an assignment for you."

The supply guy was a younger man about my age. He was also in civilian clothes and told me he had worked for the company a couple of years. He'd been in the navy for a hitch and was going to college on the GI Bill. There wasn't a great selection of uniforms available, and we could only find one that fit me. It hadn't been cleaned by the last wearer, and had big sweat stains under the arms. He told me not to worry, to check back with him in a few days because there was a constant turnover of personnel, and there would probably be a better selection later. Then he took my fingerprints, mumbling something about it being a Texas state requirement.

"You got a gun, Wade?" the personnel man asked me when I went back to his office. I told him I didn't but that I could purchase one if need be. I asked him what kind of weapon the company wanted me to carry.

"We kind of leave that up to the individual," he told me.

"Some men already have their own equipment, so we aren't too finicky about it. You'll need your own leather, too. Get black rather than brown because it goes with the blue uniform better. Sit down and let me tell you what I have in mind for you."

He told me that a rich banker in town had received a couple of anonymous death threats, and he wanted an armed guard outside his house at night. "It's a simple job, Wade," the personnel man told me. "You just drive over there to his house at six in the evening, guard the place, and at six in the morning you go home." I said it sounded OK to me, and he told me that if I had an hour or so to spare one of his field supervisors could take me over to the house right then, introduce me to the live-in housekeeper, and let me look the job over.

It turned out that this rich banker lived in a mansion surrounded by about 10 acres of virgin woods in an exclusive part of Houston known as the Post Oaks section. I looked around at what I considered to be the "area of operations," made a few mental notes about what kind of equipment I'd need and how I'd "accomplish the mission," and then met the housekeeper and told her I'd be back the next night to assume my duties. The field supervisor, an elderly, white-haired gentleman who wore a uniform with captain's bars, told me he'd be around now and then to check on me at night and then he cut me loose. It was only then that I realized I hadn't even thought to ask what the job paid.

First thing I did was drop the uniform off at a one-hour dry cleaners; then I went shopping. You have to remember that I'd just gotten out of 10 years in Special Forces and had been back from Vietnam for only a few months. I figured I knew exactly how to do this little job I'd been given and the kind of tools I'd need to do it. I went to the local gun store and bought a Browning High Power P-35, five extra magazines, belt and holster, a set of handcuffs, and penlight. After a little more thought I also purchased a Remington 870 riot gun that had an eight-round magazine extension, a pistol-gripped stock, and combat sling.

It was already getting dark the next evening at six o' clock when I checked in with the housekeeper and told her I was on duty outside. I made my last-minute preparations to go to work. Besides the guard uniform, I was wearing a pair of jungle boots I'd liberated from the army. On my head I wore a black navy watch cap, and to cover up the shiny guard badge on my shirt, I'd slipped on a camouflage jacket. I loaded the shotgun alternating buckshot and slugs, double-checked the pistol to make sure it was locked and cocked, and just before I faded into the woods that surrounded the house, I smeared charcoal on my face, neck, and hands.

For the first two nights I patrolled around the house the way I'd learned to do in the army. I scouted all the trails and other likely avenues of approach to the place, and found several locations where I could watch things without being seen myself. It was chilly, damp, and miserable, but I was used to that sort of thing. Besides, all I had to worry about was interdicting one or two possible murderers, not a horde of blood-crazed Viet Cong.

It was foggy and rainy on the third night, so I was being especially vigilant because of the lowered visibility. About two in the morning I was sitting in my favorite ambush spot near the front of the house by the driveway, when I heard a car stealthily turn in to the property. When it came into view I immediately saw that it was just the old field supervisor from the company coming around to check on me. He stopped the car right next to where I stood, still undetected in the dark woods, and started shining his flashlight over toward my parked car.

I stepped up next to his side window and quietly said, "Hi, captain."

He jumped about a foot off the seat, gasped, grabbed his chest, and appeared to be going into cardiac arrest. When he got back to normal he peered at me standing there in the rain, armed to the teeth and sopping wet.

"Son," he said, "come on around here and get in the car. We need to have a little talk."

When I got in next to him he turned the heater up a notch or two and asked me whether I'd ever worked in private security before. I told him I had only done it in the army. "Look, Wade," he said. "Here's the way it is. You're only making minimum wage on this job. All you are expected to do is show up on time, sit in your car, and try to stay awake until morning. You aren't supposed to hide, you are supposed to be obvious. The idea is to scare away any intruders, not sneak around in the woods like some friggin' killer commando!"

Since that first assignment 30 years ago I've learned a lot about the private security industry. I've worked a variety of guard assignments and have worked at every level from unarmed part-time guard to operations manager of a major security company. By reading this book you will find out what I wish I'd known back then.

One interesting thing I've learned over the years is that there is a hierarchy in private security jobs. At the bottom are jobs that require little or no prior experience or training and are easy to get, but have low pay and low prestige. As you move up the scale, the jobs are fewer, require more training and experience, and are harder to get. Some of the higher-level jobs can get quite dangerous, also, but as you go up the scale, the pay and benefits generally increase, too.

The hierarchy looks something like this:

- Unarmed fixed-post guard
- Specialized unarmed fixed-post guard
- Armed guard
- Bouncer
- Corrections officer
- Armed courier
- Bodyguard
- Computer/information security specialist

Each chapter of this book deals with a different level of the job hierarchy. I will give an overview of each type of work, explaining what training, background, and qualifications the person doing the hiring is looking for; where to find the jobs; what the work is like; what kind of pay and benefits to expect; what chances there are for job advancement in each field; and the good and bad points of each.

At the end of the book I'll go over some different career strategies, options, and possibilities, such as getting into management, starting your own security company, or maybe getting one of those exotic, high-paying overseas jobs you keep hearing about.

CHAPTER 1

Unarmed Fixed-Post Guard

A t the bottom of the security hierarchy we find the category of unarmed fixed-post guard. This is the largest and most diverse category, and includes both entry-level jobs and those that require more specialized training and experience.

In this chapter I will discuss the industry in general, with particular emphasis on the basic, entry-level, unarmed security guard position. In the following chapter I will talk about the many unarmed security guard jobs that are more specialized and make up their own subhierarchy within the unarmed-guard category.

If you are just getting interested in security work, you may not have made up your mind about trying it or not. Here's an overview of the field to help you understand who your employers will be and what to expect in the job search process. I will also discuss the good and bad points of this level of security work, as well as what your first day may be like.

OVERVIEW

There are two main security guard employers: the contract guard company and the in-house, or proprietary, security department.

Contract Guard Companies

The oldest and probably best known contract security guard company in the United States is Pinkerton's. Founded by Allan Pinkerton in 1850, this is the outfit that was hired by the railroads to hunt down The Wild Bunch, and it was also this company that played a big part in the labor disputes at the beginning of the 20th century. However, business mergers and globalization are now the order of the day.

In 1999, Pinkerton's and American Protective Services were purchased by a Swedish firm, Securitas, thus creating the largest security company in the world. In the year 2000, Pinkerton's (Securitas) bought out Burns Security, which was another large, well-established security company, giving Securitas an even bigger slice of the pie. Currently Securitas operates in 30 countries, does $4 billion in business each year, and employs more than 150,000.

Two other big players in the contract security game are Wackenhut and ADT, both of which are American-owned international companies employing thousands of people. Any major city in the United States has numerous local, privately owned security companies, though. Here in Tucson, Arizona, for example, I counted 27 listings for contract guard companies in the Yellow Pages. In most cities today, both the large and small security companies are hiring.

Are there advantages in working for a large, multinational outfit, or would you be better off with a smaller, locally owned one? Let's take a closer look at each.

The bigger companies have strong financial backing and

aren't likely to go out of business, leaving you suddenly out of a job. The bigger companies also have plenty of uniforms and other equipment, and these are furnished free of charge. The big companies have a lot of experience behind them, which is passed down to the local level in the form of business outlines, training programs, liability requirements, and so forth, and generally this makes for a smoother operating organization. From my experience training is generally better with large companies, too. Larger companies have training departments, and these produce and distribute the latest in written training material, audio-visual equipment, training aids, and the like.

Some of the smaller, locally owned companies work on a tight budget and slim profit margin, and I know from personal experience that bouncing paychecks are not all that uncommon. Also, many small companies require that you purchase your own uniforms and equipment, and this can be a strain on your budget.

Some of the smaller security companies were started and are being managed by retired cops or ex-security people who have no background or training in business management. This mismanagement filters down to the workers, often making things hectic. On the other hand, many of the owners really care about the guards who work for them. Occasionally some security-savvy owners take the time to personally train the new guy, and if that happens you will get some good, no-B.S. education in the field. Many ex-guards do start their own companies because they are truly interested in trying to better the industry by offering higher wages to employees and better service to customers. Unfortunately, these high-minded types eventually run up against the reality of that ol' bottom line.

Proprietary Security Departments

The trend these days in business is outsourcing as much work as possible. "Outsourcing" is a euphemism for bringing in contracted workers from outside to do work that used to be done by company employees. Firms have found that they can save money, time, and hassle by contracting out security and janitorial services. So the in-house, or proprietary, guard force is becoming extinct.

Generally speaking, working for a proprietary security department is better than working for a contract company. Proprietary jobs are harder to get and most require previous police or guard experience. Although shrinking company benefits are standard these days, the benefits, pay, training, working conditions, and job security are better with an in-house security department. Yes, these jobs are getting harder and harder to find, but there are some businesses and industries that still have specialized security training and background requirements that make necessary the use of an in-house security force. I'll get into this in more detail later when we discuss specialized security jobs.

QUALIFICATIONS

It's probably safe to assume that you are just starting in security work and have little or no experience. Before you get too involved in your job search, you need to know whether you meet the minimum prerequisites to do the work. Laws governing security work vary a little from state to state, but in general you will not be allowed to work in security if you are under the age of 18, do not have a Social Security card or a foreign work permit, or if you have a felony conviction.

These days most states have a licensing program for guards, and it is most often run by the state police. The police will fingerprint you and run an agency check on you to determine whether you have any prior criminal conviction. Most states allow you to obtain a temporary guard license so that you can work in security while the background check on you is being run. Almost all security positions these days require that you pass a drug-use screening at the time of being hired, and many firms do random checks during your term of employment. Those are the minimum of requirements you have to meet down at the low end of the security hierarchy. However, any employer may have other things that it requires of a job applicant. (More on that later.) Because there are currently many security jobs available, the first thing you should do is make a list of job openings that sound interesting to you, and then decide what kinds of companies you would like to work for.

FINDING JOBS

One good way to find an unarmed security job is simply by looking in the daily newspaper. The Sunday paper is always better because it contains more ads. There is fierce competition right now for security people, and some of the ads sound almost hysterical in their need: "Thirty full-time, thirty part-time guards needed NOW! Start immediately! Uniforms and equipment furnished. No experience needed, will train! Above average pay!"

Most contract security companies don't give the names of their accounts in newspaper ads. You might read that the job is "with a high-profile account" or get a general geographical location, but you usually won't see specifically where they are. So if job location is important to you, you will have to go in for an interview.

There are other approaches to finding entry-level security openings. One way is to pick a location, such as an office complex where you would like to work, find out what guard company has the contract there, and then apply to that company. But you have to first decide whether you're willing to accept another position with the company if there are no current openings at your desired location.

Another course of action is to pick a few security companies out of the phone book that look interesting to you (maybe because their offices are close to your residence), and call them up. Simply ask whether they are hiring and, if so, schedule a time to go in to talk with them.

The standard job search practice of sending out résumés,

either via e-mail or on paper, doesn't work very well for such entry-level positions. All companies will want to interview you personally anyway, and most would rather not mess around with looking through résumés.

The next thing to do is interview with each of the companies you have picked. It is through the interview and written job application that a company decides whether it wants to hire you. There are certain things that guard companies look for in applicants, and the better you meet this profile, the better your chances of getting hired.

What They're Looking For

Appearance counts in this business. Guard companies and their client firms look for neat, clean-cut people. Although being a slob won't necessarily keep you from getting hired, it certainly won't help. Guard companies prefer that you present a "military appearance" even if you have never been in the military. Anything that tends toward the bizarre is out, and this includes facial piercing, facial tattoos, and oddball hairstyles or colors. Being overweight and in poor physical condition isn't necessarily a disqualifier, but being grossly overweight will probably keep you from being considered, if for no other reason than that there are no uniforms to fit you. You should show up for the interview in clean clothing, bathed, and with your teeth brushed. I realize that this sounds pretty obvious to most readers, but unfortunately security guard work attracts a lot of losers and flakes. Here is another hint: Those with the best appearance and demeanor will be the first picked to go to "high-profile accounts," which are the accounts that pay the best.

Another important thing that security companies look for is reliability. By reliability, I mean someone who shows up for work on time, sober, in proper uniform, and ready to go to work. I know this sounds idiotically obvious to most readers, but you would be surprised at how many workers, especially the younger ones, find these requirements onerous.

This is probably a good time to emphasize the importance

of punctuality. If you are just starting in security, you may never have done shift work. When you go to work, you will be relieving one of your fellow employees when you get there, and that person is not allowed to leave the post until properly relieved. If you want to make an enemy for life, just start showing up 10 or 20 minutes late every day, especially if the person you are to relieve has already been on post for 12 hours or so. Also remember that if you don't show up for work on time, or at all, and don't warn someone in the company about it in advance, it causes a lot of hassle all around. The person who is on post waiting to be relieved will start calling in to the office, the office will start trying to get in touch with you to find out what's going on, a field supervisor might have to go relieve the person on post until a replacement for you is found, and so on and so forth.

You'll need to convince a prospective company that you have reliable transportation and a home phone: two basic requirements for employment in the industry. In some large metropolitan areas with good public transportation systems (New York City, for example), having your own car isn't as big a deal as it is in a city like Houston or Los Angeles. In most areas of the country, however, if your only means of getting to work is public transportation, bicycle, or walking, the posts and shifts the company can assign you to will be limited. A security company also wants to know that it can get in touch with you by phone in case it needs to pass information on to you, or to find out why you fail to arrive at work on time.

Don't come across as a job hopper, even if you are one. I once read someplace that the average employee turnover rate in private guard companies was on the order of 800 percent per year. In the company I worked for as a manager, it seemed like our turnover was 800 percent each hour! This is a big problem for the industry, so even if it is not the place for you, give the impression that you plan to work the job for at least 90 days.

What You Should Look For
When you receive an employment offer from a company,

don't make a commitment until you have had a chance to check out all the companies on your list of possibilities. During interviews with the companies you should find out what you can about such important concerns as pay and benefits, job assignments, and whether or not they issue uniforms at no cost to you. What is your general impression of each company? Does it seem organized? Is its office clean? Are its uniforms plentiful and in good shape, or are they worn looking? Talk to some of the company's guards. Are they happy with their jobs?

Here are a few more hints you will find helpful when choosing a company to work for. First of all let's talk some more about that matter of pay—which can vary by as much as several dollars an hour among companies. Some companies pay the same rate for all posts (accounts), but many base their pay scale on the amount the client company is paying them for the service. Remember that each client account was picked up through submitting bid proposals, so each contract with the guard company is different. The standard in the industry is to pay the guards one half of the amount the security company receives from the client company. This means that if the guard company has a contract that pays it $11 an hour for the service, the guards themselves will earn around $5.50 per hour. Usually, if you are just starting out, the company will assign you to one of its lower paying accounts. But if you are quality guard material, you have a good chance of starting at a higher rate.

Some companies will want you to start as an "on call floater" who fills in for those unreliable guards when they fail to show up for work. This means that you must be available to go to work at any time and that you have no choice in what post you are sent to. Avoid this setup if the company only offers a low pay rate. The current practice in most companies is to pay the floater a fixed rate that is higher than any of the accounts the company services. Becoming a floater is usually considered a step toward a supervisory position.

One final thing you might want to be careful of is the reputation the security outfit has with the local cops. This isn't as big a problem as it used to be when I first started working private security, but it still exists. Most of the friction between "real" cops and security guards is caused by young guards who are cop wannabes and who overstep legal bounds. Things usually don't get troublesome with unarmed guards working fixed posts on private property, but when the security people are armed it can lead to conflicts. Many police take an elitist attitude, especially when it comes to their rights to carry firearms on the job. When street cops come in contact with wise-ass armed security guards (whom the cops consider to be ill-trained, poorly disciplined, slovenly, and probably stupid, to boot), sparks often fly. This is especially true when the armed security people are operating as patrolmen, running a route on the streets. If the word is out among the local police that the company you work for is no good, you can expect a lot of harassment on the job. About the only way you can find out whether or not a guard company is on the blacklist is if you have a friend on the police force who will tell you about it off the record.

Your First Assignment

When you're a new kid on the block, a security company will probably offer you one of its least desirable posts, correctly figuring that you won't know any better. Posts can be undesirable for a number of reasons.

The first thing that can make a post undesirable is that the guard company underbid the job, resulting in pay lower than normal. Try to stay away from jobs that pay only minimum wage even if you are just starting out. The fact that you are even reading this book shows that you have more on the ball than the average starting security guard, so try to bargain for a better paying position. At the time of this writing, today's job market indicates you have some leverage.

Some jobs are undesirable because they are too far away, and this boosts your commuting expense to an impractical level. Some jobs are undesirable because they are in dirty, hot, cold, or otherwise uncomfortable locations. A common example of this might be a gate at a large construction site or mine entrance. I, myself, once worked for a major company in Houston that had a contract with the city government to guard the wastewater plants. The pay for these posts was above average, but the places stank to high heaven and no one lasted there very long.

And, finally, there are posts that are undesirable because they are too damned dangerous to be working at as a poorly paid unarmed guard. These jobs include such locations as sleazy trailer parks and apartment complexes, all-night ATM machines in the bad part of town, and the parking lots of dance joints or roadhouses. I have numerous experiences with these types of assignments, so let me share a couple with you.

Once when I was younger and stupider, I worked one of the floater jobs I told you to avoid. I was sent to fill in for the regular guard at a drive-in barbecue and beer joint in the roughest part of town. I spent four of the worst hours of my life there with my back to the wall, smiling a lot, and trying to stay alive. While I was there, two police officers in a squad car came cruising through and called me over to the car window. First they asked me whether I was trying to commit suicide. They told me that the regular guard who worked the joint was a six-foot-six, 280-pound professional bodybuilder and martial artist. And, although it was supposed to be an unarmed post, the cops said they knew that the other guy always carried a hideout gun as a backup just in case. They also told me—with a laugh—that they were afraid to get out of their car when they made their mandatory check of the place each night. I was being paid minimum wage for this.

Even though I'm older and wiser now, I still occasionally get stuck with some horrible assignments. Just a few years ago, I was living up in Oregon and doing some part-time security work to help make ends meet. For a couple of months I was posted at the local stock car racetrack on Friday and Saturday nights. The place served beer, and two or three times a night I was forced to break up drunken brawls. I went through several uniforms. This job paid just over minimum wage.

Of course this kind of excitement might appeal to some of you younger guys and gals, so if this is the case, have at it!

Once you have picked a good company to work for and accepted the job offer, you will go through in-processing. This usually involves a series of briefings in the branch office that cover your pay, benefits, job safety, uniform-wearing requirements, and general information on how the company expects you to perform your duties. If you don't have a security guard license or a temporary permit, you will be sent to the proper agency to get it. Most of the larger guard companies pay any fee requirements, but many of the smaller companies will make you pay them yourself.

In addition to the fingerprinting required for the guard card, some companies take a set of prints for their own files, along with ID photos for a company ID badge and the file. Also, at this time you will be required to produce a urine sample to be drug tested, and some companies will also ask that you take a preemployment physical. Many security companies require that you pass a standard written test that is supposed to determine your honesty. Most companies no longer require polygraph tests for low-hierarchy, unarmed security work, but these are standard for some of the higher level jobs covered later in this book. Of course, all the above mentioned tests and licensing prerequisites must be successfully passed before you are considered a full employee.

After your briefings and testing you will be issued your uniform or uniforms. Usually you will have some say in what the company gives you to wear, and you should pick the newest, best looking outfit available. Try it on to make sure it fits. Most security guards prefer uniforms that are a little large rather than those that are too tight. Remember that these are work clothes, not formal dress uniforms. If you are working only part-time, the company will probably only issue you one or two sets of pants and shirts, but if you are working full-time you should try to get at least four sets. If you are lucky, the company will also furnish a uniform jacket or coat, tie (if mandatory), and belt. You will have to furnish your own footwear, although some companies will reimburse you for safety shoes or boots if they are an OSHA requirement at your job site.

If your post assignment wasn't previously worked out as part of the hiring process, you will now be told where and when to report for your first shift. You will also probably be given the name of the person you will be relieving, a map or instructions of how to find the job, and phone numbers you can call in case you have trouble finding the location. The company will more than likely have you report for duty early that first day for training and orientation.

Specific training for each post takes place on the job, and in most cases doesn't last more than an hour, although at some more complicated guard posts the process may take a week or more. Some posts may require that you take an approved, basic first aid and CPR class. The larger guard companies usually pick up the expense for this if it is a job requirement, and the really good ones pay you overtime while you attend the classes.

THE GOOD POINTS

Today, in any medium or large city in the United States there are many security jobs available. All you have to do is find one in the want ads in the local newspaper. The Sunday paper has the most ads, and reading them is a good way to keep track of what's going on in the world of local security guard companies.

Most of the jobs listed in the newspaper are entry-level positions that require little or no experience. The company will furnish what little training is necessary and it won't cost you anything. Because there are so many openings, it is usually possible to find just the work days and hours you need, especially if you are looking for days of the week and times that are out of the norm.

Most security companies employ part-time workers, and

weekend-only assignments are plentiful. If you hate to com-
mute, it is usually easy to find work sites close to where you
live, but in some cases this will take a little shopping around
at different companies. Job hopping and working for the short
term are common in the industry, and although they put a
strain on management and supervisors, they have become
accepted evils.

Unarmed entry-level security work is usually uncompli-
cated and stress-free. Men and women do equally well in this
occupation (except for some specialized areas), and in the
past 20 years or so, sexual discrimination has pretty much dis-
appeared. The work is physically undemanding, making it a
good choice for the physically disabled. It attracts many
retirees and students, and most companies encourage both to
apply. Students can usually find quiet posts, which allows
them to study and do homework while on the job.

Applicants for security work are screened more thoroughly than for most other jobs, so you can be pretty sure that
your fellow workers aren't ex-cons or drug addicts. I've found
that you run into an interesting variety of people in this
industry, some of them bright, well educated, and with
impressive backgrounds. Unfortunately, you also find some
that fit a common stereotype, and I will have more to say
about them later.

Finally, there are many advancement opportunities at the
lower end of the security hierarchy. If you have a little prior
experience or show an interest and willingness to learn the
business, it is fairly easy to move up into a field supervisory
slot or even into a salaried management position.

THE BAD POINTS

Topping the list of things we all love to hate about private
security work is the low pay. There are several reasons for the
low pay in the security industry, but the main one is nothing
more than that ol' bottom line. The rule in business is to
spend as little as possible on such necessary, but loathed,

expenses as housekeeping and security. Client companies almost always go with the lowest bidder for a security guard contract, and this is what keeps pay and benefits low. This is simply a fact of life down at the lower end of the security hierarchy, and I don't foresee its ever getting any better. Although some of the larger security companies offer health, life, and retirement benefits, the premiums are so high and the pay so low that few workers can take advantage of them.

Just about all security-related jobs involve shift work. Many positions must be manned 24 hours a day, seven days a week, and the ones that don't go 'round the clock are in operation after normal business hours during the night, weekends, and holidays. The few nine-to-five Monday-through-Friday shifts that are available are traditionally given to those with seniority, although there are exceptions to this rule that I will talk about later.

Because of the odd hours and work schedules, a common prerequisite for employment is having a home phone and a car. Some companies will accept alternative means of reliable transportation such as the city bus or even a bicycle, but in many locations this isn't feasible. One of the reasons companies want you to have access to reliable transportation is so they can depend on your getting to the job on time.

Another reason companies want you to have your own car and phone is that they want to be able to call you at two in the morning on your day off and ask you to drive 20 or 30 miles across town to fill in for some jerk who didn't show up for work! And this brings up the unfortunate fact that although many of your fellow employees are as trustworthy as you, security work also seems to attract a lot of losers. The difficulty of having to work with these scumbags is one of the worst parts of the job, and it can get to be a real pain.

There is little or no job security at the lower end of the hierarchy. The company not only can—and will—transfer you from post to post and shift to shift at the drop of a hat, but you also may be let go without warning. Usually your employment contract will state that the company can fire you without having to explain itself at all, and you can get the boot for everything from such major infractions as theft to minor things like slovenly appearance and sleeping on the job. I know of a guard who was fired because an employee of the client company complained that "the guard never smiles."

There is no prestige in unarmed security work. In most office buildings or other facilities where you work, the security office will be found in the basement next to the janitor's closet. In most organizations, the only department lower on the food chain than security is janitorial. Many employees in the client companies will treat you with disdain and downright hostility if they happen to have problems with authority figures. Your friends and neighbors won't be very impressed with you either, except for the occasional 5-year-old boy who sees the uniform and thinks you are a real cop.

A part of the job that drives some people crazy is that many work assignments are mindless, boring, and seemingly senseless. Often the hardest part of your job, especially if it's at night, is staying awake. Getting caught asleep on the job is one of the great bugaboos in this occupation and can get you fired on the spot. Oddly enough, as soon as you advance from simple guard positions to even the lowest level of supervision, the work loads and stress levels increase dramatically. In the salaried positions, work weeks of 70 hours are common, and you will be on call 24-7. Unfortunately, the pay levels don't increase at the same rate as the workload, and this is why there are so many promotion and advancement opportunities available.

YOUR FIRST DAY ON THE JOB

Let's briefly go through what your first unarmed guard shift might be like. We'll say that the job is at a large office building and your post is at the main employee entrance. Your shift hours are Monday through Friday, 4 P.M. to midnight.

You arrive an hour early as instructed, find a place to park, and report to the day guard who is manning a desk just inside the rear door. You notice that this guard looks pretty sharp, and he or she might even be wearing some form of rank insignia. This is because guard companies try to put their best people on during the times that there is heavy person-to-person contact with the client's personnel.

After introductions, this guard will give you a quick run-down of your duties, show you where the written post orders are, and tell you what forms and paperwork you are required to do each shift. This is minimal, usually just a log sheet of activities for each shift. You will be given a quick tour of the building, shown where the bathroom and breakroom are, and told of any specific doors you are to lock or areas to check during your scheduled security rounds. The guard will then wish you luck and leave, glad to be getting off work 45 minutes early.

Your trainer has told you that your job is to check ID badges as each employee enters the building, to lock the door at 4:30 P.M., to unlock the Dumpsters for the janitors at 10 P.M., and to make one security and fire check of the building between 10:30 and 11 P.M. In the meantime, your job is simply to man the desk and unlock the door for employees who come back to the building for some reason. Any employee you let in after hours must show you an ID badge and sign the after-hours logbook. At midnight your relief will arrive and you go home.

Things run as planned during your first shift. All the employees have left the building by 4:15, and you have smiled pleasantly at each and mumbled a "good evening" to each as you were instructed. The janitors arrived, did their jobs, and left right on schedule, and you finished your tour of the building in less than 15 minutes. You begin watching the clock moving toward midnight, and the time starts to drag. When it's finally quitting time, your scheduled relief hasn't arrived! You wait 10 minutes, and still no relief. You call the guard company dispatcher on the phone and inform her of the problem. She tells you to hang in there, and hangs up. At 1 A.M. an exhausted-looking field supervisor from the guard company arrives in a company car and relieves you of duty.

You have just finished a typical day's work as an unarmed security guard.

CONCLUSION

Working as an unarmed fixed-post guard is an unglamorous, generally low-paying job, but the work is easy to find and may help you get your foot in the door. In the next chapter we'll look at jobs that are a little bit more specialized, more interesting, and probably higher paying.

CHAPTER 2

Specialized Unarmed Fixed-Post Guard

N ow I will talk about some specialized jobs in the unarmed fixed-post category. The pay for these jobs increases somewhat, and the work is a little more challenging and interesting. As I mentioned in the first chapter, due to the specialized training required for some of these jobs, often they are with in-house security departments rather than with contract guard companies, and this is always considered a step up in the hierarchy.

Here is a list of such jobs, not necessarily all-inclusive, pretty much in order from lower to higher on my scale: airport security, government building security, hospital security, hotel security, retail security, casino security, and labor disputes security. Let's take a closer look at each.

AIRPORT SECURITY

If you have flown anyplace in the past 20 years or so, you have had to go through the metal detectors and baggage X-ray machines to get to your gate. Since the terrorist hijackings of four commercial airliners on September 11, 2001, the job of airport screener has come under great scrutiny and has been the subject of much hand-wringing by lawmakers and the media. As I write this in early October of 2001, what the future holds for these jobs is still unclear. Some in Congress want to take the jobs completely out of the private sector and federalize all screeners. President George W. Bush's plan is to keep the screeners privately employed, but to give responsibility for training and managing them to the feds. Everyone seems to be in agreement that the screeners should be better paid and better trained. All I can say to this is: Well, duh!

The work that security personnel do at airports primarily involves screening passengers and their baggage to detect dangerous items such as knives, guns, and bombs. This job requires that you be on your feet for most of your shift, and that you are able to interact with many different types of people under sometimes tense and confrontational situations. The job requires enough basic knowledge of technology to operate the metal detector and baggage X-ray machines. You will also work with a variety of local, state, and federal police agencies responsible for air terminals.

Prior to the terrorist attacks of 2001, the pay for airport security screeners varied from city to city, but in general was at the lower end of the scale. I'll take this time to reemphasize a point about the pay in the private security industry: A company will pay you as little as it can get away with. If the company is having a hard time filling all its contracts, then the pay scale will tend to creep upward. The pay scale for these jobs may also rise if they come under federal control.

The basic requirements for this work are the same as those for all guard jobs. The perfect applicant for this job is the usual clean-cut individual, male or female, with a pleasant, non-volatile personality. This job applicant should be near middle age, in good health, not excessively overweight, and with no physical impairments that prevent standing for eight hours at a time. A good work background for the job would be other security work that required heavy face-to-face interaction with the public. Other preferred backgrounds include having worked at something like grocery store checkout clerk or at the complaint desk of a department store. In my experience, little old ladies who look like someone's grandmother are excellent in these jobs. The further you are from fitting this description, the less likely you are to do well in the job, although not meeting all the dream-applicant criteria isn't necessarily a disqualification. You can also expect more thorough background checks for screeners in the future, and this may delay the speed with which you can actually start work.

Before the heightened emphasis on security, only 12 hours of training were mandated by the Federal Aviation Administration for the job of screener. Most real training was done on the job. In the future you can expect many more hours of required training.

Several contract guard companies specialize in airport security, and before the terrorist attacks they didn't seem to advertise their vacancies much in the want ads. Since the attack I've started to see more ads. From what I've gathered from talking to airport security people, the turnover of employees is high. Probably your best bet to get one of these jobs is simply to go to the airport, talk to one of the guards there, and ask where you should apply. There is a good chance that the guard company has an office right there at the airport, so be prepared to fill out the job application and to interview on that first visit. If these jobs eventually come under federal control, you can expect to fill out a lengthy background investigation form, so have all the requisite information with you.

My guess is that the chance for advancement in one of these jobs is very good, especially if you have a little supervisory background, good people skills, and prior security experience. The guard company will be looking for people who can interact with the public, the police, other employees at the terminal, and with other guards. If you move into a first-line supervisor's position (equivalent to foreman), expect a pay increase of 10 to 20 percent over the standard guard pay rate. If you move into something like site supervisor, you should expect and demand a substantial pay hike because you will be earning it.

I've already touched on some of the undesirable parts of this job, and I'll get back to those in a minute. Here are a few features of airport security that many guards I've talked to seem to like. First of all, the work is indoors, so you will be warm in the winter and cool in the summer and won't get wet, muddy, or dirty. You are busy most of the time—there is a lot of activity going on in airports around the clock—so your shift will probably seem to pass quickly. It is a good job for female security officers who might feel vulnerable to assault at more isolated posts. You are doing obviously important work because, as everyone now realizes, the possibility of terrorist acts against airlines is very real. Many take security jobs at airports in hopes that they might lead to some better paying airport job such as ticket agent, baggage handler, or member of the airport police department. There might be a few perks with the job such as free parking at the airport or discounts with some of the food and souvenir vendors.

Before the attacks of September 11, 2001, the worst part of working in airport security was that air travelers were stressed to the breaking point. Flights were often overbooked, there were numerous cancellations and delays, and the planes were crowded. As of this writing, however, air traffic and travel are down. Instead of stress from overcrowding, we now have the stress of increased security screening and the fear that people have of getting on an airplane at all.

As a security screener, you are in uniform—an authority figure—and although travelers now understand and even welcome the inconvenience of screening processes, you will have to deal with a lot of aggressive, disgruntled people. A typical stress-inducing situation is one in which a passenger already late for a flight must be delayed because he set off the metal detector. Of course you are backed up by the airport police, federal marshals, and other armed-and-ready individuals, and, if things get too out of hand, the unruly person can expect to be hustled off to the security office and might even end up in the slammer. As I said, airport security is serious business, these days more than ever.

GOVERNMENT BUILDING SECURITY

Most government buildings outsource their security requirements to contract guard companies. Federal buildings require armed guards, but city, county, and state buildings are generally guarded by unarmed personnel. Due to several shootings in court buildings and the recent threat of terrorism, these now have metal detectors at the doors and people who enter must be screened the same as they are at airports. Besides the possibility of terrorist acts, most government buildings are in city centers, and in many large cities the downtown areas are home to various transients, lowlifes, scumbags, and substance abusers, all of whom also pose potential threats.

The job of securing government buildings is similar to airport security in that there are metal detectors at some entrances. There is more attention to the physical security of the buildings themselves, however, and depending on the setup, some jobs might be outside on the perimeter of the building and around parking lots. The buildings are secured 24-7, with more guards required during normal business hours than at other times. During the day shifts, there is heavy interaction with both government employees and the general public.

Expect the night shifts to be quieter. The metal detectors usually are not in use, and the work mostly involves such things as manning sign-in/out logs for after-hour employees, making scheduled fire and security rounds inside the building, and chasing away the occasional street person who might try to urinate in the doorway.

As with airport security jobs, most of your training will take place on the job. You can probably expect more required training in the future; however, much of it is related to countering the new terrorist threat. Many contracts with government agencies now require that the guards be qualified in basic first aid and CPR, and if this is the case you will be scheduled to attend this training at a later date. If you work for a decent company that has negotiated a fair contract with the client, this training is paid for by the guard company and you are paid to attend the training.

In most cases the pay for these jobs is a little better than average. Often, especially in more politically liberal cities and counties, laws are in place that require all low-level government jobs to pay substantially more than the minimum wage. In the past few years, however, there has been more emphasis on cutting back government budgets, so more and more you will find that the jobs don't pay any better than any other contracts the guard company has. Here in Tucson, for example, some of the lowest paying guard jobs in town involve government contracts. As with the job of airport screener, however, people are realizing the importance of these jobs, and one can hope that the pay situation changes for the better in the future.

Besides meeting the basic qualifications for any guard job, the successful candidate should have many of the same traits as those required for airport security. Because a lot of the work in these jobs is performed during the day directly in the public eye, guard companies look for those much valued, but hard to find, clean-cut individuals. As with airport security jobs, people skills are important, especially if you are posted at a metal detector station. Although many of the street-people types you will be required to confront are harmless and unaggressive, be aware that some are real nut cases, so having the physical ability to either escape from them or defend yourself might be an issue.

I've been told by people in the know that most government contracts for outsourced security services are routinely rotated among the competing companies. The reason I was given is that the service provided is always best at the beginning of the contract period when the guard company is trying to make a good impression, but after a while it deteriorates. Because the government agencies change guard companies so often, it is pretty easy to find a job. Guard companies tend to worry about getting the contracts first and finding the workers to fill the contracts second, so there are almost always large advertisements in your local paper screaming and begging for help. Or you can take the obvious step of visiting your local court building, asking one of the guards there which company he works for, and then applying to that company. While you are talking to the guard, ask him whether he likes his job and whether the pay is any good.

Once again, the prospects for advancement to a first-line supervisor's job are pretty good. Previous supervisory experience and some prior security work might immediately land you a supervisory slot at the time of hire, especially if the guard company has just won the contract and is trying to fill all the new slots. Expect the usual 10 to 20 percent increase in pay for doing first-line supervisory work. Do a good job, let it be known that you are interested in further advancement within the company, and when the site supervisor quits or gets fired, you might get his job.

Here are a few good and bad points of doing government building security. On the positive side there are more day shifts available than usual. This is important to many people, especially single parents who need to be home at nights to take care of their children. These are also pretty safe jobs for women to work at night because there is generally at least one other guard on the premises and it's easy to get assistance from city and county law enforcement. Since most government buildings are found downtown, it is easier to get to work by public transportation than it is for more isolated sites.

Probably the worst part of doing government building

security is having to deal with the weirdos and transients who congregate in downtown areas. As I mentioned earlier, many of these people are mentally unstable or strung out on a variety of drugs. A particular problem is that these people are usually filthy and diseased. If you have to come in physical contact with one of them for some reason, you must be extremely careful. A bite by one of these people could transmit AIDS. (Besides that, there are also tuberculosis and hepatitis to worry about.) Putting your life on the line is not on your job description for unarmed guard work! I personally don't think the threat of terrorism at county, city, and state government facilities is very great, but this is certainly another thing that you will need to take into consideration.

HOSPITAL SECURITY

If you spend a lot of your free time watching doctor and paramedic dramas on television, you would probably like doing hospital security. Because hospitals are semipublic places, access control is an important part of the job, and one of the most important jobs in hospital security is keeping unauthorized people out of restricted areas.

Because hospitals get sued so often, their administrations must be able to depend on their security forces to keep the nut cases out. A few months ago here in Tucson, there was a story in the news about a breach of security at a major hospital: some pervert had managed to get into the hospital and onto one of the wards. He donned a white doctor's coat, draped a stethoscope around his neck, and started making rounds of female patient's rooms. He was finally caught when the third or fourth patient he visited wondered why the doctor was doing a pelvic exam on her when she was in the hospital for a broken arm. Of course there are lawsuits pending, and you can bet your sweet bippy that heads rolled in the security department!

Besides access control, there is usually some troublesome activity going on around the emergency room to keep an eye on, and the parking lots must be guarded. Particular care must be taken to guard the business offices and gift shops, where cash is found. Female nurses seem to be a particularly favorite target of rapists, and one of your nightly duties will probably be escorting them to their cars when they get off duty.

Hospital security can get complicated, so after the usual one or two hours of general orientation in the office, you can expect to put in several days to several weeks of on-the-job training. In big facilities it might take several months of rotating through the various positions before you really feel like you know what you are doing.

You can expect above-average pay for working hospital security, and there are probably some fair health and life benefits. Sometimes these jobs have a probationary and training period of several months, during which you there is a lower starting wage. At the end of that period the pay increases by 10 to 20 percent and the bennies kick in.

Requirements for doing hospital security are more stringent than for airport or government buildings. Hospitals have many liability concerns, so they have to take care that their own security people don't add to the problems. Because of the special nature of hospital security, these jobs are often with in-house security departments rather than contract guard companies. For these reasons hospital security should not be considered an entry-level security job. Usually prior hospital security experience is a prerequisite for hire, but depending on how desperate a hospital security entity is to fill a post, it might also consider people with generalized security experience. This is another job that requires a lot of contact with the public, so the ability to deal with a variety of people—some of them under great emotional and physical stress—is important.

People of both sexes and all ages can work successfully in hospital security, with the little-old-lady types handy for consoling upset relatives of patients and the young, burly males good for ejecting trespassers and escorting pretty nurses to their cars at night.

Hospitals usually advertise their openings in newspapers, but sometimes they list them only with state-run job centers or depend on word of mouth. The usual tactic of visiting the hospital and applying at the personnel office might be fruitful. Because this work is specialized, having a résumé already printed up will be helpful. If they don't have a current opening, you can tell them you are interested in working there and ask that your résumé be put on file. The human resources person might actually look through this file the next time there's an opening. Your chances are even better if you can talk directly to the head of hospital security, especially in an informal social setting.

The chance for advancement in hospital security is pretty good, especially if you have quite a lot of previous security experience and have worked in hospitals before. In general, however, there are fewer advancement opportunities with proprietary guard forces than with contract companies because the turnover isn't as high. If you are just starting work at a hospital, expect to work about a year before you start politicking for advancement.

There is never a dull moment in a large hospital complex, and this is what many people like about the work. After all, we are talking about life-and-death situations and all they entail. Hospitals work around the clock, of course, and, as with government building security, there are plenty of daytime shifts available for those who need or prefer them. There is certain mystique about working around large, bustling hospitals (just look at the popularity of doctor shows on television). For those who might be planning to become emergency medical technicians, nurses, or even doctors, working security at a hospital is a chance to see what goes on firsthand.

But if you are like me and hate going to the doctor and have to be dragged to the hospital to visit even your closest dying relatives, this work isn't for you. It is also said that hospitals are the dirtiest places to work because there are more potentially harmful germs, bacteria, and viruses floating around hospitals than anywhere else on earth. One of the jobs you may be asked to perform as a hospital security person is physically restraining wild, unruly patients who may be thrashing around due to medication, illegal drug or alcohol intake, pain, fear, or any number of other reasons. This person might be some old woman who reminds you of your mother, or it might be some 19-year-old gangsta punk full of drugs and gunshot wounds. In either case, you face the chance of catching something (AIDS, for example), getting accidentally hurt yourself, or of hurting the patient. And as for me, I've been around enough hurt and dying people in Vietnam to last me the rest of my life.

HOTEL SECURITY

Hotel security has a lot in common with hospital security, and about the only reason I put it higher in the security hierarchy is that it seems more romantic to me. I read a lot of detective books when I was growing up, especially the ones written in the 1930s and 1940s by Raymond Chandler and Dashiell Hammett, and in those books the characters were always going into seedy hotels and being given the once-over by the hotel dick. There still are plainclothes hotel detectives around, but these days they are integrated into the hotel security system that includes uniformed officers, closed-circuit television (CCTV) monitors, credit investigations, and a lot more.

As with hospital security, there is always a lot of action at hotels. Like hospitals, hotels operate 24 hours a day, seven days a week. Guests are checking in and out all the time, hotel clubs and restaurants stay open into the wee hours of the morning, drunken guests are forever wandering the halls, conventioneers are raising hell, and prostitutes, con men, muggers, and burglars are all there looking to prey on the guests.

Typically, the chief of security of the hotel is an ex-cop of some sort who gets to wear civilian clothes and be a modern-day hotel dick. The chief is also usually the only one who gets to carry a gun, although use of one is seldom recommended or required. There might be a few more undercover security people posing as guests, but the majority of the security force is uniformed guards. The work is both inside and out, with the parking areas being a particular problem area. Once again ,the job requires good people skills because the hotel management doesn't like it if its security force pisses off paying guests, even when the paying guests deserve it. Usually these jobs are proprietary, especially for big hotels, but sometimes smaller, sleazier hotels in the crummier parts of town do contract with a guard outfit for partial coverage of some sort.

About the only way to learn hotel security is by on-the-job experience and training. You will more than likely receive the standard one- or two-hour orientation, then be turned over to a more experienced officer or supervisor to learn the ropes. To be a success at hotel security, you have to learn some pretty subtle skills that involve walking the line between being tough and giving ground. Treatment of guests is always touchy. You can be tougher, for example, with transients caught trying to steal luggage out in the parking lot than with obnoxious Joe Yuppie, the drunken conventioneer.

Hotel security pay is variable and depends a lot on which city, whether the job is proprietary or contracted, and how the job market for security people is at the time you are hired. If you have previous experience working hotel security, or if you have some law-enforcement experience, you can expect higher than average pay. Health and life benefits will be average, but there might be some perks involved, such as discounts on rooms, free or discounted meals at the hotel restaurants and coffee shops, and discounts with the regular hotel hookers—only kidding!

As at hospitals, hotel security is specialized work. Previous experience in hotel security or in other areas of the hospitality industry is always be an asset. It may be possible to get an entry-level job in hotel security depending on the current job market, how sharp you are, or if you have a good reference from a current security employee. The job can be successfully performed by men or women, and age isn't much of a factor as long as you are in good physical condition. Most of the jobs require quite a lot of walking around the hotel, the parking areas, and hotel grounds. Stairwells will have to be checked, drunken guests helped to rooms, scumbags chased, and so on.

In my experience, large hotels don't often advertise their security openings in the newspapers. A lot of jobs are filled by word of mouth and the old-boy network. If you already work for a large contract guard company, it might have some contracts with hotels that you could get assigned to, and this can give you some hotel job experience to put on your résumé. As with many other security jobs, one of the best ways to find out what's available is simply to go to the hotel you are interested in and start nosing around. Ask the human resources department first and try to talk to the head of security. If you are a good prospect, he will likely be glad to talk with you about any current or expected openings. Having a prepared résumé is a good idea.

There is a good chance of advancement from guard up to first-line supervision after you work awhile and learn the ropes. If you work for a proprietary guard department, it will be more difficult to go much higher unless someone quits or gets fired. If you have law enforcement experience plus prior experience in the hospitality industry, you could end up as chief of security. If you have a business degree, and if the hotel is part of a huge, international chain, you might even climb your way into a security-related job at the corporate level.

One of the best parts of working in hotel security is that the work environment is rather pleasant. It's better to spend your eight hours a day hanging around a fancy resort hotel than sitting at a dusty, noisy truck gate at a factory. If you are in college working your way through a degree aimed at the hospitality industry, hotel security can give you some firsthand experience with the work. Or, if you are interested in some other hotel employment, such as desk clerk, security might give you the connections you need. As with hospital security, there is always something going on at a hotel, so it's not as easy to get bored as it is with some security jobs. There is a challenge in catching grifters, prostitutes, and professional hotel burglars—plus there is the possibility of those perks I mentioned.

One of the worst things about working hotel security is that you are constantly in a damned-if-you-do, damned-if-you-don't situation. Loud, obnoxious guests must be handled firmly or other guests will complain, but the loud, obnoxious guests will probably file a complaint with hotel management that they were harshly treated. At the least you will have to be verbally reprimanded, and you might be fired. Remember, there is no job security in this racket.

RETAIL SECURITY

Two reasons I place retail security so high on the scale are that, first, much of the work is in civilian clothes working undercover and, second, trying to outwit shoplifters is challenging and fun. There are several levels at which you might work in retail security. These days, most large stores have several layers of security. First there might be overt, uniformed security officers working out in the parking lot, posted at the customer entrances and exits, and possibly back at the shipping and receiving docks. The uniformed officers might actually be from a contract guard company. Inside the store are the plainclothes store detectives who pose as shoppers and keep an eye out for shoplifters; these are usually in-house security people. Somewhere in an inner sanctum will be banks of television monitors that are attached to numerous CCTV cameras, and other in-house security personnel will be monitoring these during business hours. Besides trying to catch shoplifters, retail security also has the responsibility for trying to stop theft by store employees, which in some stores is the biggest cause of so-called inventory shrinkage.

You will probably receive a fairly lengthy training session before starting the job because there is a lot to know about catching shoplifters. Also, maybe more important, there are some big-time liability concerns you have to become familiar with before you start busting suspected shoplifters. There is some on-the-job training, but it's hard to teach undercover work while actually doing it. Catching shoplifters seems to require a certain knack, and this is only developed through experience.

You should expect better than average pay for store security, especially if you have prior experience and a proven track record of catching thieves. If you work for the store's proprietary security department, you can expect the same benefits and perks that the other store employees get, such as health and life insurance, paid time off, and possibly a discount on merchandise.

It's kind of hard to get into retail security unless you have some prior experience, but some stores will hire a sharp trainee, especially if the person has prior law enforcement or general security training and experience. Any other retail experience is helpful, especially if you had worked around such high-risk areas of a store as the jewelry or electronics departments.

Women do especially well as store detectives for some reason, maybe because so many shoplifters are women! Also, during the day, in any large department store, the majority of the shoppers are women, so female undercover operatives blend in better.

There are no particular physical prerequisites for the job, other than being able to stay on your feet for long periods, negotiate stairs quickly, having good eyesight, and possibly knowing how to defend yourself if one of your collars goes ballistic on you. Also, a store detective needs a certain amount of aggressiveness to be successful. If you already have an interest in this line of work, you probably already have the kind of special personality it takes to do the job well.

I don't see many ads for store detectives in the newspaper. If you are interested in this kind of work, try making the rounds of the big stores in your area, drop off résumés, try to talk to the people in charge of security, then check back with them now and then. If you already have some connections in the world of private security, use them to look for openings. Also ask people who work in other departments at stores you are interested in to find out whether there are any openings or pending openings in security. The best time to look for jobs in retail security is a month or two before Christmas. Sometimes you can get a temporary job even if you have little or no experience, and this might work into something of longer duration. You will also have better luck finding a retail security job if you are willing to work evenings and weekends, because those are peak shopping times. Tip: Don't just look at department stores for work. Many large grocery stores now have security departments, especially those that sell liquor and have pharmacies and branch bank outlets.

The more specialized security work becomes, the fewer the opportunities for advancement. Depending on how large the security department of a store is, there are probably one chief of security and, possibly, three lead security people. As with all security work, though, there is a large turnover in retail security work, so your best bet for advancement is to simply stick around, learn all you can, show an interest in the job, and work your way up through the ranks.

As I mentioned before, one of the best parts about retail security is that it is kind of fun to match wits with shoplifters. Catching the professionals is always a real challenge, although most of your trouble will come from amateurs who decide to steal on the spur of the moment. Most people in security think that getting to work in plainclothes is a plus, the same as moving from patrolman to detective in a police force. You will be working indoors, in climate-controlled conditions, and you will stay clean and dry. Many people just like being in big stores and malls, especially women, so they find the work environment enjoyable. Once again, there will probably be some perks involved with the job, such as store discounts.

As with hotel security, you have to be careful when handling customers—and God help you if you make a false arrest. Most stores these days use hidden television cameras extensively, and monitoring these can be boring to some people, especially to those who would rather be down on the sales floor prowling around trying to catch someone. (The other store clerks and employees might be leery around you since they know that you are also watching them!) Some stores want to occasionally use their security people for other duties, such as stocking, running the cash register, and general flunky work, and this can lead to misunderstandings and hassles.

CASINO SECURITY

Now that casino gambling on waterways, Native American land, and other specially designated areas is so common around the country, casino security isn't as specialized as it once was. This security is very much like retail security in that there are layers of security that include uniformed and undercover operatives and CCTV monitoring. Casino security focuses a lot on catching gamblers trying to cheat, but because of the large amounts of money handled, the casino employees are also closely monitored.

Modern casino security is very technologically sophisticated and depends heavily on surveillance cameras, both to catch fraud and stealing on the spot and also to videotape records of everything that takes place in sensitive areas such as money rooms. The Mecca for casino security is still Las Vegas, where some amazingly whiz-bang techno security stuff is taking place. As mentioned, there are different areas of security you might be in, including uniformed work, undercover work on the casino floor, or work as a surveillance officer who monitors the CCTV screens.

Training is mostly of the on-the-job variety. While much of the security at casinos is pretty straightforward, such as patrolling parking lots, escorting customers to their cars, and guarding money, security personnel have to learn the many rather esoteric secrets and techniques that gambling cheats use.

These must be learned along with other job-specific security routines and procedures that the casino might use to keep its employees honest.

Pay and benefits for casino security are usually well above average for security work. Here in the Tucson area, casino security work pays about twice the going rate for other unarmed security jobs. Once you get experience in this specialty, you might even be able to earn a living wage, something that's a rarity in the security industry.

Qualifications for the job depend a lot on what part of the casino security system you are working. Looking good and having a military bearing are more important if you are in uniform and working in the gaming area than if you work upstairs monitoring television screens. If you are on the floor working plainclothes, you can and should look like no one in particular. Six months to a year of prior security or police work is usually preferred, but because casino security is so specialized, prior knowledge of the gaming industry usually isn't a requirement for entry-level jobs. If you happen to be an experienced card sharp or have other arcane gambling knowledge, you can probably get a job as some sort of advisor to the security department. If you are applying to work at a Native American casino, Indian employment preferences are in place, but this doesn't mean that only Native Americans need apply.

Casino jobs are regularly advertised in the newspapers, and if you are near Indian land and there's gambling there, drop off a résumé and ask to fill out an application. Most casino security is run by in-house, proprietary security departments, but they might also contract some of the uniformed work out to various guard companies. Of course, the best place to find these jobs in the United States is in Nevada or Atlantic City, and if you are really interested in this kind of work, that's where you should head. But you have to keep your eyes open; many areas that you wouldn't immediately think of as gambling centers now have casinos along their waterways or in specially designated areas. Donald Trump owns a casino on Lake Michigan in Gary, Indiana, and there are several casinos in the mountains of Colorado.

If you are not of Native American descent, your best chances to advance in casino security are in Nevada. If you *are* of Native American ancestry, though, you can have the best of both worlds: Learn the job and move up as high as you can on your home turf, and then take your training and experience and go hit the big time in Las Vegas.

I haven't personally worked in casino security, but it seems exciting and interesting. As in retail security, there is the challenge of matching wits with professional thieves, con men, cheaters, and other such characters. Also, due to the huge amounts of money generated and processed, there are internal fraud and employee theft to watch out for, and the constant possibility of armed robbery attempts! If you like doing security work, it doesn't get much better than this. Finally, if you are fond of gambling, why, after every shift you'll have your chance to drop a few quarters into one of the slots.

From talking to some present and past casino security people and from doing similar work, I know that one downside to the job is the heavy requirement for monitoring those CCTV screens. This can get to be really tedious, and you have to stay on the ball and not let your attention drift, especially when you are trying to catch the very subtle motions of sleight-of-hand artists. Some people, even if they have no real moral qualms about gambling, eventually get worn out by the whole atmosphere in a typical casino. I think that being a dyed-in-the-wool cynic is probably a personal requirement to work in the industry. As in retail security, there probably exists a strained relationship between the security department and the other employees. I had a good friend who was a card dealer in Vegas for several years, and he said after a while he really got tired of being observed constantly while on the job.

LABOR DISPUTES SECURITY

There is one more form of private security service that I'll mention here in the unarmed fixed-post chapter, simply because I don't know where else to put it. Ever since the end of the 1800s, business management has hired private security people to side with them during disputes with labor. Pinkerton's was heavily involved in this area back in those days, not only by furnishing armed and unarmed guards to protect the physical facilities themselves, but also by infiltrating labor groups to spy on them.

Tensions have simmered down a lot between management and labor recently, and the level of violence during labor disputes (strikes) isn't nearly what it was in the past. However, there are several security companies that specialize in labor dispute security, and you will occasionally run across ads in the help wanted section for security people to work a strike.

Labor dispute security can get physically violent; there is the possibility of getting seriously hurt from fists, clubs, thrown items, and even gunshots. The pay for this type of work is right up there at the top of the security guard scale, and because of the inherent danger it is exciting work. It's because of all this that I place this type of security work at the top of the unarmed fixed-post hierarchy.

Unless you work for a security company that specializes in labor problems, the jobs are of a temporary nature. Usually, security personnel for this work are recruited from a different location than where the problems are taking place. This is to reduce the chance of the security person having a personal relationship with someone involved in the strike. Security companies that specialize in this work travel all over the United States, and one company I'm familiar with is Falcon Global, so I presume it is prepared to work worldwide.

If you work a labor dispute on a temporary basis, after you are hired you'll travel with a group of other security employees in transportation provided by the company to the location of the strike. Usually there are living arrangements for you right inside the facility that you are to protect, and you will be required to stay there for the duration of the job. These living arrangements are Spartan, usually just cots, with food either prepared for you there, brought in through the picket lines, or in some cases merely something like military combat rations.

Labor dispute security work involves protecting the physical facility from vandalism (up to and including the building or buildings being burned to the ground), conducting general riot and crowd control, and making it possible for vehicles to enter and leave the premises. The vehicles may contain your daily rations, management personnel, or the scabs being brought in to do the work of the strikers. Expect to be recorded on videotape a lot. Not only will management and the security company record everything you do, but so will the strikers and the news media. Also expect to spend some days in court after it is all over testifying in lawsuits and counter-suits from both sides.

If you work for a company that specializes in labor disputes, you can expect some good training. You will train as part of a team in riot control techniques and equipment, first aid, communications, and the use of video cameras. If you are doing the job as a temporary employee, you will probably be given a crash course in these same subjects.

As I mentioned, you should expect top dollar for this kind of work, along with free food and a place to sleep while on the job site. Because this work is dangerous, you should also expect some free health and life insurance benefits, and the health insurance should cover any long-term care you might need after the job is over.

The company that hires you for this work will look for a person with experience in riot and crowd control, either in the military, police, corrections, or private security. Usually the security company is more inclined to want you if you are big, strong, and ugly—seriously. Big, strong, ugly guys are more intimidating, and are the norm for this work—which is why the striking workers usually refer to the security force as the goon squad. This aspect, as well as the communal living conditions, means that women, even with prior experience and training in police and corrections, won't have a good chance at these jobs.

If you want to work for a company that specializes in labor disputes, check the Internet. Run a simple search using key words and phrases such as labor dispute security, labor crisis management, and goon squads (only kidding on that last one). Once you find the firms' points of contact, send them your résumé with a cover letter telling them why you want to work for them. You will probably have to relocate if you are hired. If you are interested in temporary work, keep your eyes on the local newspaper. The employment want ad for the job will tell you very little, but will probably say up front that this is for a labor dispute, tell you that it is temporary and out of town, and probably mention a pretty good sounding per diem pay rate of something like $150, with a minimum guarantee of 10 days' pay.

Companies that specialize in this work are usually pretty close-knit. Once you get some experience with one, however, and indicate that you plan to stick around, you should be able to move into a first-line supervisory slot (Goon Squad Leader, lst Class?). With the temp jobs, of course, you will be in and out quickly, although you might get something like a battlefield promotion if the strike lasts a long time, if it is particularly violent and bloody, and if there are lots of casualties on the guard force.

The good parts of this job are the high pay and the camaraderie that comes from working as a team and doing a dangerous job. Once you get inside the company facility you are guarding, you will be surrounded by a screaming mob of people who hate your guts and it will feel like the last days of the Alamo—or maybe Khe Sanh. I have never worked for a company that specialized in labor disputes, but I worked a short contract as a temp, and there was a definite elitist feeling among us troops.

One of the worst parts of working these jobs is that you might feel like you have more in common with strikers than you do with the fat-cat owners. If you come from a blue-collar background and your father is a retired union member, you won't want to do this work. (If this is the case, you will more than likely be screened out in the pre-employment interview anyway.) Also, the work involves being away from home for an indefinite period, having a real chance of getting hurt, and being considered the villain by many people. If you fought in the Vietnam War you will know what I mean.

CONCLUSION

This concludes a whirlwind trip through the world of unarmed fixed posts. We started at the bottom of the security hierarchy with generalized, entry-level security guard jobs and worked our way up the ladder to some of the more interesting and challenging positions you might find. Again, this list isn't meant to be all inclusive, and some of you who already have experience in security work might argue with my ranking of the jobs. But most experienced security people will agree with most of what I've said. In the next chapter I will take you to the next level of the hierarchy and start talking about a very serious aspect of security work: guns and the possibility of killing.

CHAPTER 3

Armed Security Guard

With this chapter we get into serious stuff, not only because this work might involve life-and-death situations for you and others but because of the huge liability concerns for you, personally, and for your employer.

Before we go any further, I want to take some time to get on my soapbox and talk a little about guns and their use by average citizens, armed security professionals, and police agencies. First of all, so you will know where I'm coming from, let me give you my personal background with firearms.

I started shooting at the age of 5. My father, who spent his life in military and police work, was a gun enthusiast and was my instructor until I joined the U.S. Army at age 18. I have spent most of my adult life in jobs that involve the use of guns. I'm still an avid shooter and

National Rifle Association (NRA) member, and of course support the Second Amendment to the Constitution. Having said all that, I have to also tell you that from my experience there are many people owning and carrying guns who have no business doing so. This includes the usual bunch of gangsta punks and other criminal types, but also more than a few concealed carry-permit holders, security guards, and police.

Way back when I first got involved with private security work, an old, cynical guard supervisor told me this: "Wade," he said, "there are two kinds of people doing this work. There are young, cop wannabes who want to carry around a chrome-plated pistol and act tough, and there are old men who want to do as little as possible." Training, licensing, and certification in the security industry have improved a lot since then, but that statement still has a lot of truth to it.

Now before any of you elitists who work for police agencies start nodding your heads in agreement, I need to remind you that this same statement often applies to "real" cops. Although police firearms training has improved over the years, most police only fire their weapons during required qualifications. I've heard many horror stories over the years about police ignorance of firearms. A friend of mine who works at a gunshop and shooting range told me one about a detective who brought his revolver in for maintenance. Seems that the cop needed to clean his gun, but couldn't get the cartridges out of it. My friend said that this old cop had been carrying a nickel-plated, J-frame Smith & Wesson close to his body. It hadn't been cleaned or fired in such a long time that half the nickel had peeled off, and the cartridges had corroded in the cylinder and had to be driven out from the front with a punch and hammer.

Another story I heard from a different gunshop owner (you can see where I spend a lot of my spare time) was about the cop who brought in his revolver wrapped in a towel. The cop had drawn his weapon and cocked it, but then couldn't figure out how to get it back into a safe condition. "If I pull the trigger, the gun will go off," the cop said, and because the cylinder wouldn't unlock while the gun was cocked, he couldn't unload it.

I spent my army career in Special Forces and could tell you many more stories about improper gun handling and ignorance of weapons that I've seen among some supposedly trained troops. Once, as a joke, just before he was due to hold guard mount inspection I asked a young lieutenant whether I could look at his .45. I detail-stripped the weapon and handed the pieces back to him in his beret. He was still trying to put it back together 10 minutes later when it was time for him to fall out for inspection.

There are many of you out there, both young and not so young, who think that putting on a gun makes you invincible. You think that because you are wearing a gun people will be impressed and give you more respect. Although you might impress an occasional old lady or young kid, in reality when you are wearing an exposed weapon as a security guard, it only makes you a prime target.

When you are an armed guard you pose a serious, immediate threat to possible assailants, which means that during a holdup or a terrorist attack you will be the first one taken out! I know this for a fact from talking to many armed robbers while I worked for the Federal Bureau of Prisons, and also from my own training and experience with special operations units while I was in the army. It's just common sense. Think about the last movie you saw that portrayed a bank heist. Who was the first person the robbers did in? That's right, it was the old geezer of a bank guard who never saw it coming. Killing a rent-a-cop doesn't carry the same punishment as killing a real cop; all professional criminals know this, and terrorists couldn't care less whom they kill to accomplish their mission.

Although many guard companies reserve their armed posts for more experienced people, many other companies will hire people with no firearms training or experience. Some companies require that you go through their in-house firearms course and then successfully pass their qualification course. Some states also require an armed guard to take a course, pass a written test, and qualify with the weapon.

Meeting these minimal requirements is not enough, in my opinion, for a person to be an armed guard. I think armed security personnel should have more training. There are several things you can do to get this training; two good places to get some reliable firearms training are the military or various police agencies. Obviously, you will get better weapons training from the military if you are in something like an infantry or military police unit rather than if you are a cook or clerk typist.

Of course, most people aren't going to run out and join the marines just so they can learn to shoot. These days, there are lots of good firearms training programs available for civilians. You can start by taking some basic courses that the NRA runs. Next, if your state has a concealed weapons-carry law, take the training required to get a license. As a next step, you could attend one or more of the various combat-shooting schools now offered all over the United States. Some of the best known are Gunsite in Arizona, Thunder Ranch in Texas, and the Lethal Force Institute in New Hampshire. These shooting schools all offer multilevel training, starting with basic stuff and advancing into training that is as intense as most SWAT-team members get.

Proficiency with firearms is all about practice. Shooting is like any other athletic skill in that it deteriorates with time. If you carry a gun professionally, you need to stay in practice. This means you should be dry-firing (practicing with the unloaded weapon) daily and doing actual live fire on the range at least once a week.

I know that this sounds like a lot of hassle, time, and money, but we are talking about saving your life and the lives of others. Some of the better security companies that require their guards to be armed will pay for some of your practice ammunition, and maybe your range fees as well. I shoot often because I enjoy it, but when I'm working an armed-guard post, I try to range-fire two to three times a week.

Here is another good piece of advice. If a job requires that you carry a gun, it also requires that you wear body armor. We are talking Kevlar vest here, what is commonly referred to as a bulletproof vest.

In the past 20 years there have been great improvements in this area. In the old days, the vests used metal plates and chain mail of various configurations to stop the bullets. These old types were really heavy, bulky, and could only be worn under something like an overcoat. Back in the late 1950s and early 1960s Kevlar vests were introduced. Some of you will remember the old flack vests issued during the Vietnam War. These were lighter weight and easier to wear, but were still bulky and had to be worn as an outer garment. Not too long ago, an outfit named Second Chance came out with the now common lightweight vests that can be worn under clothing.

Although the latest generation of body armor is a big improvement over the old stuff, it is still hot, fairly heavy, and uncomfortable to wear. Most police departments and armed courier companies (which I will have a chapter on later) recommend, but don't require, that their people wear vests. Even though as a private security officer you will probably have to bear most, or all of the cost for a good Kevlar vest, I certainly recommend you purchase and wear one while on duty. Although you can expect to pay $300 to $400 for a Kevlar vest, what price do you put on your life?

The kinds worn under clothing are popular because they aren't as obvious. The sales slogan of Second Chance is, "If they see the body armor, they shoot for the head." Since you will purchase the vest yourself and probably work for several security companies during your career, the concealed vest is also better because the color won't have to match your uniform!

OK, that ends my sermon. Now let's take a general look at armed security work.

OVERVIEW

Thirty years ago, when I first got involved with private

security, it was common for contract guard companies to offer an armed roving patrol service. The people assigned to this detail were the best the guard companies had because not only were they armed, but they also drove company vehicles. One of the main jobs of these patrols, which were equipped for radio communications, was to check on clients who had burglar alarms and to respond to the alarms should they go off.

Due to liability concerns, armed roving patrols aren't as common as they once were, but some companies still offer this service, and if you are interested in working armed, this is something to look into. It can get pretty hairy, though, because on an alarm call you will often beat the police to the scene, if they come at all. It will be up to you to determine whether a burglary is actually in progress, has already occurred, or is merely a false alarm.

In recent years governments at all levels have outsourced many of their security needs. Since the attacks of September 11, 2001, the advisability of putting so much faith in low-paid, often semitrained, and unenthusiastic private guards has come into question. As with airport screeners, you can expect to see more government oversight of these jobs in the future, along with better pay and training.

As I mentioned in the previous chapter, federal buildings use armed guards. The job of securing government buildings is about the same whether you are working armed or unarmed. There are metal detectors at entrances that must be manned, building security rounds to be made, and so forth. Especially since the Oklahoma City bombing and the new war on terrorism, there is more emphasis on the terrorist threat. A close watch will be kept on the outside of the building for unattended bags or packages lying near the walls, rental trucks parked just outside the front doors, and guys wearing ski masks, carrying automatic weapons, and screaming in Arabic.

Besides in the federal buildings in downtown locations, the government also uses armed contract guards at other locations. There are strict security rules and regulations that must be followed by defense contractors, and these regulations require armed security. Often these guard forces are in-house, proprietary outfits, but sometimes the work is contracted out to a guard company. Remember, proprietary guard departments are almost always better to work for than contract companies. If you live around a large aerospace manufacturing plant, chances are good that the guards there are armed and well trained.

There are some interesting job possibilities here. Ever read those supermarket tabloids about flying saucers and such? The infamous Dream Land, or Area 51, is a huge hunk of desert in Nevada where top-secret research and development are conducted. From what I gather, part of the security force for this complex is provided by Wackenhut Corporation, which over the years has begun to specialize in lucrative, high-profile, government security accounts. Evidently, the Wackenhut guards protect the outer perimeter of the facility and apparently spend much of their time chasing away flying-saucer nuts who try to sneak in to get a look at what the government won't tell us about aliens. If this is true, then the Area 51 guards are well trained and well paid.

Other work for armed guards can be found at nuclear power generator stations. These are hot spots not only because of the possibility of terrorist attack, but because they are popular places for various groups to hold protests, vandalize, picket, and generally harass. I'm sure I don't have to go in to any detail about the horror that would be unleashed should one of these facilities be blown up by some nut case. Most of the security at these facilities involves guarding the inner and outer perimeters, providing access control, and making sure that all security rules and regulations are followed. The guards at these installations already receive some of the best training and highest wages in the industry, but you can expect to see more emphasis on upgrading these jobs in the future.

One of the oldest jobs for armed guards, which dates back hundreds of years, is protecting money! Where you find lots of cash you will find hired gunmen guarding the loot. There is something kind of mercenary about this that appeals to me.

When I'm acting as an armed guard hired to protect some rich person's money, I think of myself as part of that old tradition that goes back to the armed caravans, kings with their paid retainers, and all the rest of it.

Banks are places where you used to find armed guards, but you see fewer and fewer of them there now. These days, banks depend on video cameras, exploding dye packets in money bundles, and a new, nonviolent philosophy of appeasement. Nowadays it's, "Give 'em the money and don't do anything that might excite the bastards and cause someone to get hurt!" This is too bad, because many an old retired cop used to earn some extra money doing these jobs.

Jewelry stores and pawnshops get robbed a lot, especially the high-end ones and the ones in poorer neighborhoods. Both kinds of establishments use armed guards, as do special events such as gem shows and antique auctions. Usually just the presence of a uniformed armed guard is enough to make a potential robber go elsewhere and find easier pickings. But remember what I said about you being the first target should a robber, or gang of them, decide the size of the take is worth their risk and your life.

Gambling casinos and horse racetracks are also places that handle a lot of cash. I talked a little about casino security in the previous chapter and mentioned that you would find both uniformed and plainclothes security operatives there. Usually casinos and racetracks use uniformed armed guards to protect money rooms and to escort large amounts of cash transferred within the facility.

There are many other smaller, possibly temporary or part-time jobs for armed guards that turn up. Once, in Oregon, I worked a three-day gig as an armed guard protecting the money at a small carnival run by a charitable organization. I had another one-night job as an armed guard at a college fraternity party. Generally speaking, working armed will get you better working conditions and more interesting jobs than working unarmed. For example, at the carnival job, the unarmed guards had to check tickets, hassle with gate-crashers, kick out drunks, and break up fights. All I had to do was guard the money and be prepared to have a shoot-out if necessary.

TRAINING

Twenty or 30 years ago armed security guards could expect no firearms training at all, and very little training of any other kind. Guard companies would try to hire people with military or police experience or simply make armed guards out of anyone willing to do the job. We can be thankful that those days are fading fast. (Liability lawsuits—not the good intentions of security guard company management—have been the main cause of this turnaround.) These days you can expect to receive anywhere from a few hours to a few days of weapons training. Some of it is classroom lectures on such topics as use of deadly force, and some of it will be on the range trying to train you well enough to pass the company's basic shooting qualification course. The good companies pay for your range fees and ammunition. Most companies require you to qualify at least twice a year, or base their frequency of requalification on the local police requirements.

This firearms training will be with the sidearm you carry on the job (probably a company-issued weapon, and probably a revolver) and may be with other weapons, such as the riot gun. Many guard companies also offer training in unarmed combat, use of pepper spray and the baton, and handcuffing techniques. This additional training is often reserved for its armed officers because they are usually considered the elite officers of the guard force. You might also expect basic courses in first aid, cardiopulmonary resuscitation (CPR), and a lecture on the current dangers of contamination by blood-borne pathogens, such as the AIDS virus.

PAY AND BENEFITS

Armed posts should always pay more than unarmed ones, even if you are doing exactly the same work as the unarmed guard. Contract guard companies always demand that their clients pay a higher rate for armed guards, and the client companies expect this. The better contract guard companies pay their armed guards at a higher rate than their unarmed guards regardless of the account the guard is working, and whether or not the account *requires* an armed guard. Other companies might only pay their armed security officers at a higher rate when they are assigned to an armed post. It's that ol' bottom-line bugaboo again, folks, and you might as well get used to it.

Some armed posts actually involve quite a lot of risk, especially when you are protecting a site that has a high probability of armed holdups or terrorism. It is a sad—but generally true—fact that in this industry, the crappier and more dangerous the job, the less they want to pay you to do it.

Often these dangerous jobs are of short duration, such as during a period of civil unrest and riot. I remember seeing some scenes during the last riots in Los Angeles that featured some tough-looking Korean security guards. In one film clip, one of these guards was shown ripping off five or six rounds out of a Glock. I don't know whether he hit his target or not, but I hope so.

You will usually have some leverage as far as pay for these short-term, extra hazardous assignments. For your own good and every other private security officer in the industry, you should demand top dollar for this work. If you are an armed officer and work an especially dangerous guard post, you should also try to negotiate better than average health and life benefits for the period you put yourself at risk. Ask for a rider on the standard policy that gives you a private room instead of a bed in the open ward, and at-home nursing care while you are convalescing. You also might want to ask for some dental care that covers dentures if you get your teeth knocked out by a brick or baseball bat.

QUALIFICATIONS

It's harder to get a job as an armed security officer than to get work on an unarmed post, and this is one of the main reasons I place it higher on the scale. Contract guard companies and in-house security departments have higher hiring standards for armed guards than for unarmed. Employers will want you to have experience in one or more of the following jobs: military, police, corrections, or a year or so of previous work as a private armed security guard. They are going to look a lot closer at your personal history and background, especially for jobs around sensitive government facilities. Signs of instability, job hopping, poor credit, and a bad driving record will probably keep you from being employed. Your driving record is especially important if you are being considered for an armed security patrol route that involves use of a company-owned vehicle.

This is a good time to emphasize prior job experience. From this level of the hierarchy on up your work history becomes more and more important. And as I said before, experience in the military, police, or corrections is most highly regarded. Think of this as a core requirement. In my opinion, based on my experience in the industry, the best prior experience is with the military.

When a job applicant for a security job has successfully completed a period of military service by receiving an honorable discharge, the hiring company can assume that the applicant already knows how to wear a uniform properly, understands personal grooming standards, has a good work ethic, understands the concept of chain of command, and is punctual and dependable.

The former military person is also familiar with guard duty, and it is hoped at least remembers the part of his general guard orders that stated that he will not leave his post until properly relieved. The applicant who's been in the service will have had some training and experience with firearms. And, finally, the employer can assume that at least while the applicant was in the military, he or she wasn't doing drugs or getting in too much trouble with the law and maybe had received a security clearance.

Prior police experience is also a common core requirement, but many private security companies complain that ex-
police don't make very good private security officers. There
are several reasons for this.

- Police officers have a lot more power than security guards,
  and they tend to develop a cop attitude. Many ex-cops
  have a hard time remembering that when they are working as guards, they no longer have this power.
- Most police officers have little or no respect for private
  security guards, so when a cop ends up in the private security sector, he or she usually brings a feeling of superiority
  and often does not fit in well with the rest of the guards.
- Many ex-cops have done part-time security work while
  still on the police force. But off-duty cops doing security
  work are paid approximately 10 times more than regular
  security guards. So when these ex-cops find themselves
  having to work for $10 an hour instead of their previous
  $100 an hour, it often causes resentment.
- Rent-a-cops take a large ration of crap from the people
  they are guarding, and ex-police often can't handle this
  with tact.
- Most ex-police officers are doing security work because
  they are retired from regular police work. (If a former cop
  applies for a guard job, the first thing the company had better ask is why the ex-cop isn't still a policeman.) These
  retired cops have a reputation for being especially lazy for
  some reason, possibly from spending too many years sitting
  in police cars, and they don't work out very well in security
  jobs that require a lot of walking, stair climbing, and such.

Former corrections officers actually make better private
security guards than street cops, because corrections work
deals a lot with physical security of buildings and facilities.
Corrections officers also have learned to take a large amount
of verbal abuse on a daily basis, and aren't as likely to fly off
the handle at a casual wisecrack as many ex-cops are.

With both former police and corrections applicants, though, the hiring security company can assume the same punctuality, knowledge of uniform and grooming regulations, and familiarity with firearms as they can with former military personnel.

The requirements for licensing or certifying armed security guards vary from state to state. In most states, a business owner or his employees can lawfully carry firearms as long as they remain on the business property. In some states, you can work armed security with the same guard card as you do other security work. In states that issue concealed-weapons permits, you must often obtain one of these in addition to the basic license.

More and more states require a special license or permit to work as an armed officer. I obtained an armed guard license in Oregon a few years ago and it required a fee and passing a written exam that covered the legal use of deadly force and firearms safety. I also had to qualify with my sidearm on a course of fire directed by local police. This qualification course was based on the old practical pistol course, which most combat pistol shooters are familiar with, and the passing score wasn't all that high. At least half of the 15 or so people shooting with me that day were abysmally bad shots and failed the course. Now please refer back to the first part of this chapter.

FINDING JOBS

From this level of the security hierarchy on up, the old-boy network becomes more and more important. Although there is a big turnover of personnel at the lower levels of the industry, those who do this work professionally eventually get to know one another. Many people in security work have prior contacts with military or government police agencies, and if you work in private security for a few years in one city, you will develop a local reputation. This reputation can be either positive or negative, and if the word gets around that you are a slimeball, you will eventually find it very difficult to get even the lowest level security job.

Because the United States has become such a litigious country, all companies—including guard companies—are scared to death of being sued, so they will take extra care in selecting people to hire as armed guards. For this reason many armed positions, especially the better ones, aren't advertised but are filled only by personal recommendation through word of mouth.

You do, however, see many ads in the papers for armed patrolmen and armed guards, especially from contract guard companies. Often these ads are come-ons or bait-and-switch setups. At the time of this writing, employment is high and security companies are having a very hard time finding qualified applicants. Many people who know a little about security work know that armed posts pay more than unarmed, and there are also the wannabes, police rejects, and weirdos who think carrying a gun at work would be "cool." So, like used car salesmen, some security guard companies run ads claiming they have many armed-guard vacancies when in fact they have none, or only one or two. Once you go in to apply, you find out that you must start as an unarmed, on-call, fill-in for minimum wage and work your way up, or some such B.S. If you are already licensed and qualified as an armed officer, and have prior training and experience in the public and/or private sector, then mail or fax the advertising guard companies a résumé. If they really have opens to fill, you might get a call for an interview.

You might also register yourself with various private and government employment agencies. Often I've found that companies with government contracts are urged to list their job openings with the state's employment commission. Also, these employment agencies do some prescreening and prequalifying of applicants for the hiring companies, and usually filter out the obviously unqualified applicants before they are sent for interviews. I've never come across a specialized employment agency that acts as a clearing house only for security jobs, but there are probably agencies somewhere (on the Internet, for example) that provide this service.

Because of liability concerns, many of the largest contract guard companies no longer offer any armed-guard service. I was talking to a manager of one of the larger contact companies about a year ago, and he told me a horror story related to why his company no longer offered armed-guard service. It seems that this company had supplied an armed guard to a convenience store in the slum area of a major city. While the uniformed armed officer was on duty in the store one night at about 11 P.M., a teenager grabbed a six-pack of beer from the cooler and ran out of the store with it. The guard yelled, chased the kid out into the parking lot, and shot the young shoplifter in the back, killing him. Lawsuits are still pending.

The best place to look for armed work is with the smaller companies, some of which specialize in high-quality armed security. Many of the companies that specialize in high-quality armed guards are owned and run by retired police who fill most of their posts with off-duty cops. If you are well qualified to work as an armed guard and have a positive reputation in the local old-boy network, then you too have a chance for employment with these companies. Just remember, though, that the choice assignments will probably be given to the owner's police buddies.

Here is a basic job search strategy. Write up a résumé, making sure to stress any military, police, or armed-security experience. If you are already licensed or certified to do armed-guard work in your state, be sure to include this information. If you have any good personal references from such people as police officers, security professionals you have worked for, or prominent members of the community, put these on the résumé also.

Next, make a list of companies that might hire armed guards. This includes many of the local contract security companies and companies such as Defense Department contractors. The addresses and phone numbers can be obtained in the Yellow Pages of the phone book or online. Especially when dealing with large manufacturing companies, call and ask for the name of the chief of security and the proper mailing address, then send your résumé addressed directly to this security manager. When mailing to the smaller contract guard companies, you can address it to human resources or maybe the operations manager.

Mail out your résumés and wait for results. If you get little or no response, get your hair cut short, shine your shoes, put on clean and pressed clothing, and start making the rounds of the places in person. In today's job market you should be employed by the end of the day.

JOB ADVANCEMENT POTENTIAL

Unfortunately, there probably isn't as much chance for advancement in armed, as opposed to unarmed work. This is mainly because there are fewer overall openings for armed guards. If you work for a proprietary guard force at a facility doing Defense Department work, for example, there are probably only three first-line shift supervisors, one site supervisor, and, somewhere up in the mists of management, a guy or gal in a suit who has overall responsibility for safety and security. The first-line supervisors know they have it dicked and tend to stay in their positions until they die. Unless you have an MBA, are a retired colonel, and/or have a daddy as senior vice president of the company, you can forget about being the security manager.

A paradox in this business is that if most of the guard force is unarmed, then often the only people authorized to carry guns are the supervisors and managers. But when all the rank and file carry guns, the supervisors and managers often aren't armed. I suppose this is some kind of status symbol thing.

THE GOOD POINTS

One of the best things about working armed posts is that

you get paid more. If you work as an armed guard now and aren't getting more money than the rest of the unarmed guard force, then you are being suckered. Armed guards usually earn about 50 percent more than unarmed. As mentioned earlier, some contract guard companies pay this higher rate no matter what post you are assigned to, armed or not.

By accepting the responsibility and meeting the requirements to work as an armed guard, you show that you are serious about this work. Companies are more likely to foot the bill for advanced, exotic training opportunities that the unarmed guards won't get. Some of the large, in-house security departments might even pay part, or all, of your college expenses so long as you study something that will make you a more valuable employee.

You receive a little more respect as an armed officer, and there is a bit more prestige involved. If you work for a company that utilizes both armed and unarmed guards, the armed officers are considered the elite of the force. The types of work armed guards do is usually more important and satisfying than what the unarmed guards do, and this is a boost to moral and self-respect.

THE BAD POINTS

Although some people might think it's a positive point because it adds excitement and adventure to the job, the worst part of being an armed security officer is that you are in more danger of being killed or badly hurt. Unarmed guards pose little threat to assailants, and are often simply immobilized during an armed robbery. As an armed officer you will receive special attention. As I write these words, I can almost feel the testosterone surging through some of you and hear you saying, "Oh yeah? Just let 'em try to mess with me, man, I'll show the bastards a thing or two!" Yeah, right.

Besides the danger of getting killed or badly injured, there are those wonderful legal liability problems I keep talking about. If you pay any attention to the news media, you know what happens to real police when they are involved in a shooting incident. Even when shootings are obviously justified, the officers involved are suspended with pay until an investigation takes place. Even when the investigation clears the officers involved, there are often lawsuits filed. If the police have to go through all this crap every time they pull a trigger, think what you will go through as an armed guard. Even if you are totally justified in shooting, or merely pulling and brandishing your weapon, you can expect to spend time in court, possible time in jail, and may be sued into financial insolvency. Oh yeah, the guard company you work for will probably dump you, too.

If you work as an armed guard, you have to keep your licenses and certifications current. Usually this requires periodic weapons qualifications, classroom refresher training, and payment of fees. If you follow my advice, you will also need to find time to spend on keeping your weapons skills at peak level, and this involves the costs of range fees and ammunition.

A TYPICAL DAY ON THE JOB

I'm going to give you two scenarios of what a day's work as an armed security officer might be like. In the first scenario, you are working for an in-house security department of a large defense contractor. In the second situation, you are doing armed security for a contract guard company.

Example One

You are a man in your late 20s who recently got out of the U.S. Marines after spending eight years with force recon. You moved back to your hometown after discharge and went to work for the security department of XYZ Aircraft and Missile Company, which has a billion-dollar contract with the government. You have worked there about six months already and like the job well enough, but are taking classes at the local university in your spare time so you can become a schoolteacher.

There are three security shifts, each with 10 uniformed guards and a shift supervisor who has the rank of lieutenant. There is also a site supervisor with the rank of captain, whom the shift leaders report to, and a guy in a suit with the title of safety and security manager who works somewhere in the office building. You are assigned to the swing shift and report to work half an hour early at 1530 hours.

The security guards carry company-issued Smith & Wesson Model 19 revolvers and wear standard, police-style belts and holsters. Each man also is issued handcuffs and holder, a flashlight, and a small belt kit that contains surgical gloves and an airway mask. You are not allowed to take the weapons or equipment home, and when you are off duty they are stored under lock and key at the facility. The wearing of Kevlar vests is optional, and although the company docs not issue them, it pays half the cost if a guard wants to purchase one. You shelled out the extra dough and wear your vest every day, even though some of the guys think it's stupid and sometimes refer to you as Rambo.

The guard force is run along paramilitary lines, and because of your military background you have had no trouble fitting in. Your fellow workers all either have military or police backgrounds, and the shift supervisor is a retired marine gunnery sergeant who spent half his career as a drill instructor (DI) at Parris Island. Each shift supervisor holds a guard mount inspection before the shift starts and gives a daily briefing.

The briefings are never very long because nothing much new goes on at the facility. Since the attacks of September 11, 2001, you have received a daily terrorist threat level, and today this level is normal. You are told that the shop foreman has reported some tools missing, and because of this there will be a surprise lunch box inspection at the shop gate when the shifts rotate at 1600 hours. During the in-ranks inspection, you are told by the ex-DI that your one-day-old, high-and-tight haircut is a little shaggy around the ears and that your brilliantly spit-shined shoes could use a little work.

After inspection, you report to duty at the shop gate and check the lunch boxes of the departing workers. Of course this antagonizes many of them, but you answer their complaints with the usual, "Hey, I'm only doing what I'm told." No stolen tools are discovered, and after shift change is completed, you and your partner sign out one of the security department mini-pickups and make a patrol of the outer perimeter.

The facility you are guarding is in a fairly remote area and is situated on about 20 acres of land. The patrol lasts three hours and includes checking to make sure all the gates are locked, that the perimeter fence hasn't been cut, and that several outlying buildings are secure. Your partner is an old, retired NYPD cop who keeps you entertained with stories of when he worked vice back in the old days. You discover no security breaches, and by the end of the patrol you are halfway through your shift.

You next report to the main facility, where you help conduct a full security and fire inspection tour of all the buildings in the complex. Your partner has told you that these used to be called key rounds, and that in the old days the guards had to carry around a big, heavy time clock. Now all you do is swipe your ID card through an electronic reader at various locations in the plant and the information on the card, plus the date and time, are entered into the computer in the security control center.

After the rounds are completed you have one hour remaining on the shift. You man one of the employee gates and begin checking the ID cards of incoming people. Just before you get off duty there is a little burst of excitement when an intrusion alarm goes off on the roof to the research and development building. Three guards respond but report on the radio that the alarm was caused by an employee who had found the door to the roof left unsecured by janitorial, and had sneaked up there for a quick unauthorized smoke break.

At midnight your relief assumes duty at the gate, and after

locking up your weapon and equipment and checking out with the shift lieutenant, you go home to bed.

Example Two

In this second scenario, you are a 30-year-old male with prior service as a U.S. Air Force policeman and five years as a street cop in a medium-sized city in the Midwest. You have recently moved to Los Angeles and have been accepted by the sheriff's department. You won't start with that agency for three weeks, and in the meantime someone at the county cop shop has recommended you to a small guard outfit that specializes in providing top-quality armed guards.

You are assigned to guard a jewelry store in a part of Los Angeles that is the known stomping grounds of several large, teenage gangs. The store, which is owned and operated by a 70-year-old Jewish man and his 68-year-old wife, has been held up twice in the past six months and firebombed once. In the second robbery attempt the store owner emptied a Glock 26 at the two bad guys, which resulted in a blood trail out to the getaway car. The robbers had also opened fire, and a total of 36 shots were fired, which was verified by store video camera and empty shell casings. The two robbers were holding their pistols sideways in the gangsta style and hit no one, although the store owner's wife was wounded by flying glass from one of the display counters.

Several gangs have sworn to run the old man out of the neighborhood, but the store owner has been at the same location for 45 years and refuses to leave. As a child in Germany, he lost his entire family during the Holocaust. After World War II he made his way to Palestine and fought in the war for Israeli independence, then immigrated to the United States. He is a tough old geezer and claims, "The only way they'll get me out of this store is in a body bag!"

This is an obviously dangerous assignment, and you are being paid $200 a day plus full medical, dental, and life insurance. The security service you work for has issued you a blue guard uniform and a security officer badge, and you are expected to furnish the rest of your equipment and your own weapons. You work Monday through Friday, from 9 A.M. until 9 P.M.

It's 8 A.M., and you are getting dressed for work. You strap on your soft body armor over your T-shirt, making sure the trauma plates are in place, then put on your uniform shirt over that. You are armed with two pistols, both .45 caliber and both loaded with +P Hydra-Shok JHP ammo. Your main gun is a SIG-Sauer 220, carried in a Fobus strong-side belt holster. Your backup gun is also a SIG, the smaller 245 model, and you have this stuck under your belt behind your back. You also carry handcuffs, a Sure-Fire 9P flashlight, and a cell phone. At the store there is a Mossberg 12-gauge riot gun under the counter, and a good first aid kit is available.

You get to the store 10 minutes before the old man and his wife arrive to open and keep a sharp lookout for possible trouble. It's quiet this morning, as usual, because most of the neighborhood residents are still asleep after a long night of smoking crack and drinking. Once in the store, you make sure the surveillance cameras are on and functioning properly, then assume your duty position in a corner at the front of the place, across from where the old man operates the cash register. Your back is to a brick wall, and you can cover the entire store. You have a barstool to sit on, and the shotgun is within easy reach.

The day is fairly uneventful. Most of the customers who enter are regulars, people the owner and his wife know. He signals you with a slight nod that they are OK each time one of them comes in. At noon, the wife comes out from the back room where she spends most of the day, and relieves her husband for half an hour so he can go to lunch. You've brought a sack lunch with you and eat at your post. LAPD has been alerted to the possibility of further trouble at the store, and you notice a patrol car cruise by several times. At 1 P.M. the two police stop, come in the store, and ask whether everything is still all right. They strike up a conversation with you, mainly to find out if you are a pro or an asshole, and when they find out that you're an ex-cop and that you are going to work for the sheriff's department in a couple of weeks, they relax. You swap a couple of cop jokes with them, and they go on their way.

At 2 P.M. it looks as if you may get some action when two obvious gang members stroll in. There is no nod from the store owner this time. The two punks spot you right away and make a big deal out of giving you the hard once-over. After a couple of minutes of wandering around the store looking at things in the cases, one of them asks to see a large men's diamond ring. The store owner tells them that he's lost the keys to the display case. They laugh and walk back out of the store, once more looking you over as they leave. Watching them from the window, you try to see whether they get in a car, but they walk down the sidewalk and around the corner and you lose sight of them. You mark down the time they enter the store in case you or the police need to go back over the videotapes later to identify them.

At 6 P.M., the owner's wife brings you a sandwich and you eat it at your post. At 8 P.M., the owner closes up, sets all the burglar alarms, and locks the doors, and you drive with him and his wife in their new Lexus to the night depository where he drops off the daily receipts. He takes you back to your car, and your day is done.

CONCLUSION

In this chapter, we have had a look at armed security work. Hopefully, you will become a true expert with your weapons if you are going to carry them professionally. Wear body armor if you are working armed. Don't be a punk with a gun, and be careful out there!

Remember that although it can be dangerous work, armed security pays more than unarmed security. Also remember that working as an armed security officer makes you criminally and civilly liable if you wrongfully use your weapon.

In the next chapter we will look at the job of bouncer or doorman. Although this kind of work is almost always done unarmed, it is actually considered to be further up the hierarchy than many armed posts. Get ready for physical confrontations if you want to be a bouncer.

CHAPTER 4

Bouncer

T he job of bouncer goes by several other names, all of them euphemisms. Some places call them "doormen," others call them "coolers," and at other locations they might be "house security." For those of you who have led sheltered lives, what bouncers do is keep order in gatherings of people. Usually these gatherings need to have order maintained because the people are intoxicated in one way or the other, either with alcohol, drugs, rock music, youthful exuberance, sex hormones, or possibly all of these at once.

There are several reasons why bouncers are so high up on the security hierarchy scale. But the main reason is that bouncers are required to perform their duty every time they go to work. In other security jobs, such as armed guard, you might go your entire career and never have to actually pull your weapon, much less use it. Bouncers, on the other hand, have to confront unruly and sometimes belligerent people on a daily basis, and often these confrontations lead to physical violence. If you want to work as a bouncer, you definitely have to be able to walk the walk as well as talk the talk.

Here are a few other reasons the job of bouncer is rated higher on the scale. As a general rule, bouncers make more money than the average security officer. They usually work in street clothes or in a minimal type of uniform such as slacks and a T-shirt with SECURITY written on it, and most security workers like this. It is also harder to get a job as a bouncer than it is to get many other security guard jobs, so the field is more exclusive.

OVERVIEW

I believe the word "bouncer" came into the English language because when a person was ejected from an establishment by the person hired to do this, the ejectee bounced when he hit the street outside. Or maybe the unruly patron was bounced off the walls and dribbled on the floor. In any case, when people think of bouncers, this is what they imagine them doing. Actually, bouncers try not to let confrontations get to the point of physical violence. Good bouncers are able to handle situations with little disruption.

There are several different types of places and occasions where bouncers are employed. The main places that use bouncers are those that serve alcoholic beverages and attract large crowds—in other words, bars, nightclubs, dance halls, roadhouses, and the like. Depending on the number of patrons these places bring in on an average night, what kind of people they are, and where the place is located, you could have from one to 10 bouncers working every day.

Establishments that attract a primarily male clientele need more bouncers than other places. These are places such as strip joints, biker bars, and military hangouts. The age group of the patrons also indicates how many bouncers are needed.

Taverns where middle-aged guys go to drink after work aren't as rowdy as college-kid hangouts. Some places just have reputations as good places to go get in a fight. Roadhouses outside the city limits and on rather isolated stretches of highway are sure to employ a crew of "coolers."

The security forces at large gatherings with young, rowdy audiences—such as rock concerts, pro-wrestling matches, and stock-car races—will more than likely include both high-profile uniformed guards and also some bouncers. The bouncers are usually dressed for physical work in those SECURITY T-shirts and steel-toed boots (the better not to have your toes stomped on, you know?).

Often individuals or organizations that throw large, private parties hire bouncers to keep order. Fraternity and sorority parties commonly hire professionals to do this work. Any gathering that might attract undesirables or gate-crashers routinely hire bouncers.

So what exactly do bouncers do? They routinely perform several functions while on the job. One of the main duties is to man the entrance to the place they are guarding and maintain access control. In other words, they check IDs to make sure the people coming in are of legal age, or they check them against official guest lists or rosters if it is a private party, and they use their judgment to determine whether the person trying to gain entrance to the place should be allowed to. Who do they keep out? Well, the over intoxicated, the belligerent, the excessively weird, people who are bleeding and beaten up from previous fights—anyone who might disrupt order on the premises.

Other bouncers keep an eye on things inside the establishment. They watch for people who are becoming overly intoxicated, starting to act aggressively, or maybe trying to put the make on some guy's wife. The earlier the bouncer can spot the developing problem and cool the situation before it gets out of hand, the better for all concerned. Once a fight actually breaks out, people get hurt, things get broken, and the danger of lawsuits increases. (Here we are back at liability again!)

The exact timing of when the bouncer intervenes is important, and is usually determined by the type of place he works. In a bar that caters to college-age men and women or yuppies, the intervention takes place at an earlier stage of the developing trouble than it would in a biker bar, for example. In the first instance, the bouncer might hover ominously at a table where a couple of guys are simply arguing. In the second type of place, the biker bar, the bouncer might not step in until a few blows are thrown or maybe not until deadly weapons are pulled.

Once it is determined that a customer must be either restrained and/or actually ejected from the establishment, a certain amount of finesse must be used by the bouncer(s) involved. In the good old days, the bouncer might have simply sapped the offender to his knees, then dragged him to the door by the collar and given him the heave-ho out into the gutter. Guess what would happen these days if a bouncer did that? If the word "lawsuit" popped into your mind, you are catching on. Good bouncers develop tricks of the trade to handle these situations quickly, efficiently, and with as little disturbance as necessary, yet do it with minimal injury to the offending patron.

When a bouncer works at a large gathering, such as a rock concert, the situation is a little different, and can lead to even more trouble due to the size of the crowd and the general feeling of anarchy that is usually a part of these events. The security at these "happenings" is usually multilevel, with a mixture of high-profile uniformed security officers, off-duty and on-duty uniformed cops, plainclothes narks, and T-shirt-ed bouncers all working at the same time. The danger at these events is that they can turn into riots very easily, especially if the crowd gets the feeling that it is being "overpoliced," "brutalized by the system," "harassed by the man," or any other real or imagined complaint.

When working private parties, bouncers' duties are about the same as they are when in a bar or nightclub. One of their main concerns is access control to keep out party-crashers and screen out other possible troublemakers. Bouncers working a private party also probably have to be even more discrete in the use of physical force in dealing with disturbances because the invited guests are all friends of the person throwing the party and paying the bouncer for his service.

TRAINING

Most bouncers work freelance, but there are a few security outfits that specialize in furnishing "coolers" or "crowd management specialists" or the like. Sometimes the bouncer agencies are run from weightlifting gyms or are connected with martial arts schools. If this is the case, you might receive a little specific job training in addition to the normal body-building or martial arts that are already learning there. Most bouncer training has to take place on the job, however, because there is really no other way to learn all the subtleties and variations of situations you will be confronted with. For you readers who are interested in learning more about the bouncer trade, I highly recommend Peyton Quinn's book, *A Bouncer's Guide to Barroom Brawling* (Paladin Press).

PAY AND BENEFITS

Pay for this line of work is highly variable, but it should be well above what routine uniformed security work pays. As I mentioned, most bouncers work as independents, so each one will negotiate his own contract. In bars and clubs, this pay might be based on what other employees such as the bartenders, waitresses, cooks, or strippers get. You might receive a set salary plus a cut of the tips. There might be a deal between you and the owner that when you handle particularly dangerous or disruptive patrons successfully (meaning the cops aren't called and no lawsuits are filed), he slips you some extra cash "under the table." The female strippers and waitresses might personally tip you if you do a good job of keeping the mashers off them, and these tips might be in some other form than money (wink, nudge). Because you can get physically hurt and personally sued, there should be something in your contract about insurance coverage for both possibilities.

QUALIFICATIONS

Bouncers work in an interesting milieu that is a little different from the rest of the private security industry. Having a squeaky-clean background isn't as important in this field as it is in most security jobs. In fact, bouncers don't usually need security guard licenses to do their jobs in most places, and there is very little regulation at all in this part of the business. To be perfectly honest, many bouncers tend to be just a bit thuggish.

Bouncers need to be able to get the job done, and the owner of some roadhouse will overlook a few minor, or not so minor, run-ins with the law so long as the bouncer is "takin' care of business" for him. The two main qualifications to being a bouncer are the ability to fight well enough to use the exact amount of physical force to accomplish the job and the willingness to do this on a daily, perhaps hourly, basis. Liking to fight isn't necessarily a requirement, but not minding to fight certainly is.

Traditionally bouncers have been big, strong, ugly bruisers, and these are still desired qualifications for most bouncer work. The reason for this is that men are naturally intimidated by and have more respect for monsters, and will behave better if they know that's who they have to go up against if they get out of hand. Lots of bouncer work involves simply wrestling and manhandling drunks, and it's easier to do this without having to hurt the offending person if one is physically larger and stronger than the opponent.

Smaller men can also get the job accomplished—and some of the best bouncers I've known weren't huge—but they have to be very accomplished and experienced at this sort of thing. Being expert, really expert, at martial arts such as jujutsu and aikido is probably better for this work that one of the striking arts. Peyton Quinn, whose book I mentioned earlier, practices a traditional, "hard" Korean taekwon do, and uses striking and parrying techniques he has developed over the years in his work as a bouncer. He says that the quickest way to end a fight is a good solid hand strike to the head, and most men who have been around the preverbial block would agree with him. Peyton works in very tough joints such as biker hangouts, and in those kinds of places, rougher treatment is required and expected to end confrontations. If a bouncer works in a yuppie fern bar, however, he can't be blasting some Wall Street financier's head into a pink mist every time a ruckus starts . . . as appealing as this sounds.

The best background you can have for getting work as a bouncer is a proven, successful track record doing the work elsewhere. There are other types of similar work that might be substituted if you are just breaking in. Former corrections officers make pretty good bouncers, especially if they have worked in some of the tougher, more violent prisons. Correctional officers often have to physically handle unruly inmates, and they work under the same force restraints that bouncers do. Experience as a cop is pretty good, too, so long as the ex-cop remembers that he is no longer wearing a badge or gun and has no official authority. Working as a male nurse or orderly in a mental hospital could probably get you into the swing of things, too. Men who enjoy rough-and-tumble sports with lots of body contact, such as football, do well as bouncers. A background in high school, college, and especially pro wrestling is beneficial. (Many professional wrestlers and bodybuilders do bouncer work part-time while trying to break into the big time.)

The work demands that you be physically fit and in fighting trim. You don't see many old bouncers, just as you don't see many old sheetrock hangers, combat infantrymen, or pro football players. Not only is the body not up to it after a certain age, but most men tend to mellow out as they get older and lose the aggressiveness and desire to do the job after a certain point.

What about women? I've used the male pronoun exclusively in this chapter because I've never seen or heard of a female bouncer. This does not mean that there are none, or that they couldn't do the job, especially in some settings I've mentioned such as the yuppie bar or sorority party. I also imagine that lesbian bars have some tough, butch babes keeping order, but since I've never had the nerve to go inside such a joint, I can't speak from personal experience. What women have going for them is that they are often able to defuse possibly violent situations easier than men can. What they have going against them is that men aren't intimidated by women as they would be by some pro wrestler, and might tend to blow them off. Female police and corrections officers have the authority of their positions behind them, not to mention their guns; bouncers, however, have neither of these. Perhaps the best combo would be one or two women, backed up by a few hulking males.

FINDING JOBS

Using the old-boy network is the best way to find employment as a bouncer. The jobs are almost never advertised in the paper or listed at employment agencies; most jobs are filled through word of mouth. There is a big turnover in this field, though, and if you start making the rounds of places that employ bouncers you will probably be able to turn up something. You will have an easier time of it if you are 6 foot 5 and carry 250 pounds of muscle than if you are a small, nerdish-looking guy (even if you are the Grand Master of Drunken-Dragon-style killer gung fu).

You will also have an easier time of it if you have a verifiable history as a bouncer and haven't been fired from your last bouncer job for sexually harassing the strippers or half-killing some drunken businessman who pissed you off. The head bouncer will probably interview you, and he will be able to determine whether or not you are the real thing within a few minutes of conversation, so please don't try to impress him with a bunch of phony crap, exaggerations, and lies about your qualifications!

If you work out regularly at a weightlifting gym, ask around there for job leads. If you are benching 400 pounds and squatting 600 or 700 for triples without a suit or knee wraps, one of the other guys at the gym who is already employed as a bouncer might give you a lead and a reference. Likewise, if you are studying one of the martial arts, your instructor might be able to give you a job lead and recommendation if you are one of his advanced students, and if he thinks you could do the job without disgracing yourself, the school, and him.

JOB ADVANCEMENT POTENTIAL

There just ain't a lot of future in this part of the security industry. If you stick with it, after a while you may end up as the lead bouncer in a place and be responsible for the hiring, firing, and training of your crew. This could either be rather rewarding or extremely frustrating, depending on many different factors. You might start as a bouncer and eventually end up in general bar and restaurant management, if that type of business interests you. Most bouncers are doing the job until something better comes along, such as graduation from college, winning the Mr. Olympia bodybuilding crown, or marrying one of the joint's exotic dancers and going into retirement on her earnings.

THE GOOD POINTS

The pay can be pretty good as a bouncer, especially if you do a good job and have earned a reputation. Many of the earnings in the bar, club, and restaurant business are in the form of cash tips and gratuities, and can thus be kept out of the hands of the greedy IRS. You will probably be offered the same benefits package that the rest of the employees receive.

If you are interested in this line of work, you are probably young and still like to hang out in the same kind of place where you will work. If it's a strip club, you get to look at naked women for hours on end, and if it's some sort of rock concert or sporting event, you get to enjoy some of that, also. The work isn't boring, and there is plenty of action going on around you most of the time, so your shift will pass quickly. And let's face it, although there may be rules against it, bouncers often get to meet a lot of chicks on the job, both employees and customers.

Usually bouncers are free agents who work on their own, so there is a great deal of freedom and mobility. In most locations there are no state licensing hassles or fees to pay and no background investigations or piss tests to pass. (If you are a screw-up and have had trouble performing your job because of drug or alcohol abuse, the word will probably be out on you.) Usually there is no uniform to wear, although some places might require a minimal type of identifying outfit such as a red, muscle T-shirt with "No Trouble" on the front, and "No Problem" on the back.

I have to admit that there is also a certain amount of pride in being able to tell your buddies (but maybe not your mom and dad) that you work as a bouncer. It definitely gives you more status than if you are working as an unarmed rent-a-cop at an office building. Telling people that you work as a bouncer in some tough joint is also a good conversation starter at parties.

THE BAD POINTS

Although the pay is pretty good in this line of work, the other benefits, such as insurance, usually aren't much. There is very little job security either. Just screw up once or twice, hurt someone too much, or piss off the wrong customer, and you will be looking for new employment. Or if you are working in a really tough, rowdy place, then not using enough force and giving the impression of being too timid can also get you canned. Dammed if you do and damned if you don't, right?

Then there is the sleaze factor. As stated in the section on the good points of the job, some people like their working environment and status as a bouncer. Working in joints can get old quickly, however, and after a while those naked, nubile dancers are as interesting as the furniture. Having to constantly deal with assholes and drunks will eventually give you a rather sour, cynical outlook on life, if you don't already have one. You will get tired of telling punk kids with phony ID cards that they can't come in, and you will get tired of the blaring music, smoke, and general depravity.

There is the danger of getting hurt on the job, and if you get seriously injured it could limit your ability to perform future work that involves physical labor of any kind. As AIDS and hepatitis C spread more and more, any injury that involves bleeding is problematic, whether it's you doing the bleeding or an offender you are "working." Getting bitten by some drunk will send you immediately to a doctor for a blood test, and could very well lead to a dreaded diagnosis. There probably isn't much in the way of health insurance with the job, either, unless you can work something out with management.

Once again, there is the danger of being sued. Any time you have to physically handle some jerk, you set yourself up for a personal lawsuit. Depending on the circumstances, the person you eject from the premises might also file assault charges against you personally, and you could end up in the slammer. Usually these lawsuits and criminal charges are also filed against your employer, and even if both of you end up winning, your reputation in the bouncer world as a "safe-hire" is damaged forever. If you do this kind of work while waiting to get on with a police agency, you could get yourself into some kind of jam and get something on your record that might screw up your chances.

A TYPICAL DAY ON THE JOB

To give you an idea of what working as a bouncer is like, I again present two different scenarios. In the first scenario, you are a 35-year-old powerlifter trying to make a living doing strongman contests and doing bouncer work on the side in order to eat. In the second you are a 27-year-old yuppie who is a bouncer because you are into martial arts and enjoy the work.

Example One

You attended college on a football scholarship and did well in the position of linebacker until you dropped out in your sophomore year due to poor grades. You have been lifting weights since high school and originally thought you might make some money as a professional bodybuilder, but you soon realized you didn't have an aesthetically pleasing body type. After you dropped out of school, you worked construction and got serious about power lifting, where you won some major national meets in the heavyweight class. Eventually you got big and strong enough to be competitive in strongman contests, but although you scored pretty well in the last one, you still aren't in the money. At 6 foot 4 and 300 pounds you figure you are still a little too small, so you are trying to add another 10 or 20 pounds of muscle. While you train for the next contest, you work as a bouncer in a large, rowdy joint just outside the gates of a major naval base.

You like this job for two reasons. First of all, the place has a grill that makes hamburgers and chicken sandwiches, and one of the bennies of the job is that you get to eat as much as you want for free. It takes a lot of chow to keep up your muscle mass, and chow costs money. Second, unlike construction work, this job doesn't require that you burn a lot of calories, because most of the time you just stand around.

You are working the late afternoon and evening shift, and there are three other bouncers on duty with you. Two of these guys are heavyweights like you, and the third is a medium-sized guy named Fred, who has been doing this kind of work for a number of years and practices some kind of martial art you've never heard of. Fred is faster than greased lighting and you watched him take a straight razor off a mean drunk one night with no blood spilled by either man.

You report to work at four in the afternoon dressed in your work uniform of slacks and a sports shirt, and assume duty at the front entrance with Fred. The first people the incoming patrons see as they come through the door are the two of you, and the third person they see is the girl at the window who collects the cover charge. No cover charge, no get to see naked women!

The men at the naval base are just getting off duty, and many of them come directly from work to your place of employment for drinks and entertainment. You recognize most of them as regulars who cause no trouble. You mentally make a note of the few you don't know, and the one or two who, by their demeanor, you peg as possible troublemakers.

Fred has told you that in his experience these military hangouts aren't as wild as some other places. The military guys know that if they get in trouble off base it could ruin their careers, and also they usually come in groups that often include some sort of senior NCO or officer who acts as mother hen. These sailors and marines usually police themselves, Fred has told you, so if you give them half a chance they will do your work for you in case of a ruckus.

After two hours of standing by the door, occasionally shaking hands with the regulars and running off two underage college kids with fake ID cards, you have a 10-minute break. While Fred steps outside for a smoke, you go see the fry cook who has two chicken sandwiches already prepared for you.

After your break, you and Fred swap positions with two of the men on the floor. One of them tells you to keep an eye on a developing "situation" between a table of civilians and a table of submariners. You position yourself close enough to the problem tables so that they can see you, but not so close as to appear threatening. It's a Friday night and the place is packed. Exotic dancers are working on three separate stages and waitresses are circulating pushing the overpriced drinks. You notice a young marine who is bugging one of the waitresses by making lewd advances toward her, and you casually wander over and set him straight. "Hey, corporal," you tell him, "the waitresses only serve drinks. If you want something else, that's what the dancers are for." The Marine says he's sorry and gives the waitress a $10 tip. You move back over to the trouble table.

Things are getting worse between the civilians and the submariners, and Fred moves over from his side of the room to assist you in case things break loose. Suddenly things do. The men at both tables jump to their feet, and one of the civilians takes a swing at one of the navy guys. These two immediately go into a clinch, wrestle around for a second or two, then fall to the floor where they continue to fight. A chief petty officer with the navy bunch holds back his men from joining in the brawl, and Fred holds back the civilians. You step over to the two combatants, reach down and grab the top one by the arm and seat of the pants, and jerk him up in the air. At first, the guy on the bottom still has hold of him, so you have to give 'em a shake or two to break them apart.

Both fighters have ripped clothing and the navy guy is bleeding from a split lip. You inform the two of them that they will have to leave the place if they want to continue their fight, but both of them have had enough and rejoin their respective groups. This is such a common occurrence in this place that none of the other patrons pay much attention to any of it. You and Fred resume your previous positions and continue to monitor your sectors.

It's not too bad for a Friday night, and only one other altercation takes place up by the front door when an obnoxious drunk tries to get in without paying the cover charge. The two men working the door at the time take care of things with little problem. Later they tell you that as soon as the drunk got in his car, a lurking cop arrested him for driving under the influence.

The joint closes at midnight, and you've managed to gobble down four more sandwiches in the meantime. You and Fred escort several dancers to their cars because weirdo patrons have been stalking them, and when you get off work you go right to bed because tomorrow is heavy squats day at the gym and you need the rest.

Example Two

You've been studying martial arts since you were six, and at age 27 you are very good in several different styles. In college you majored in computer science, and since graduation you have made a very good living. The trouble is, you get bored easily, so when one of your sparring partners told you he was looking for someone to do some "crowd management" for him, you jumped at the chance.

The work is sporadic, and doesn't pay much of anything, but you do it because it gives you a chance to try out some of the martial arts skills you have spent years perfecting. By trial and error, you have discovered that the "iron claw" techniques work very well for this sort of thing.

Tonight at the city's main auditorium the World Wrestling Federation is staging one of its major wrestling events, and you will be working the crowd to keep order. There are several different uniformed security guard companies working, and the promoters have also hired a number of off-duty police officers. Your job is kind of a low-profile, "undercover" type of thing where you wear street clothes, mingle with the crowd, and stop people who are throwing things at the wrestlers in the ring.

You get there early and are already sitting in your sector of the auditorium before the crowd is let in. Things get wild right off the bat as a bunch of gate-crashers tries to storm through the entrance. Several of them make it in but are soon rounded up because they are easily identified by their identical make-up, which mimics their wrestling hero, The Zombie.

You are wearing a two-way radio with an earplug, and about 20 minutes into the show you get a call from a spotter up in one of the control booths. Some kid is using a rubber band to shoot bent paper clips at the ring. He tells you where it's coming from, and you immediately spot the culprit several rows away.

You work your way over next to the boy, who appears to be about 16. He is standing with a group of his pals after just launching one of his missiles, and the bunch of them are laughing like crazy. You get next to the kid and, without making a big deal out of it, casually grab him just above the elbow and sink your thumb into the pressure point there. "Hey, muthafucka!" the kid yelps, turning to look at you.

You give him another, harder squeeze, and his face loses its color from the pain. "Give me the rubber band and the paper clips," you tell him, not raising your voice and pretending to watch the wrestlers.

"Let go my arm, bastard!" the kid whines.

You give him another little tweak, and his knees buckle. "If you want to ever use this arm again," you tell him, smiling pleasantly, "give me the goddamn rubber band."

He gives it up, and you tell him that if there is any more trouble from him, he and his friends are out of there. You move back to the center of your sector as the kid rubs his arm and tries not to cry.

During the rest of the show, there are two more problems that you take care of. You spot a guy who has smuggled in a half-pint of whiskey, and you take it away from him. Not only is alcohol prohibited at the event, but so is the glass container. You also take care of a pervert who you catch trying to masturbate while he ogles one of the female wrestlers. All the incidents are taken care of quietly and efficiently, with little or no disruption.

You stay at your position after the show is over and keep an eye on the boisterous crowd until it has vacated the establishment, then you drive home in your BMW, take a shower, and try to decide what suit to wear the next day at the computer lab.

CONCLUSION

In this chapter I've tried to give you a look at what being a bouncer entails. Like many jobs in the more advanced levels of the security hierarchy, previous experience and a good track record in this specialty are important. So although your criminal and moral background might not be as important as in some other areas of security work, getting work as a bouncer can be more difficult if you are just getting started and are an unknown in the field. Remember that doing bouncer work can get you sued and/or tossed in jail if you aren't careful . . . but hey, think of all those naked dancers!

CHAPTER 5

Corrections Officer

T here is one thing to be said for corrections work these days, whether it's with county, state, federal, or private facilities: there are plenty of jobs available. I read the other day that at present there are more than two million people locked up in this country, and that number is growing. We've got more prisoners than we have prisons to put 'em all in and guards to watch 'em. This is why private corrections facilities are once again coming back in vogue.

Turning the problem of running prisons over to the private sector isn't anything new. Back in the mid-1800s this was the way we usually did it. Life in general was a lot tougher back in those good old days, but the godawfulness of those early prisons, which used the convicts as slave labor, fed them starvation diets, and routinely brutalized them, eventually caught the attention of reformers. By the beginning of the 20th century, private prisons had about died out.

Due mainly to spiraling costs the privatizing of prisons came back into fashion in the early 1980s. Originally the private sector built and ran juvenile detention centers, county jails, work farms, and a few minimum-security state units. One of the big players in the private security sector is an outfit called Corrections Corporation of America (CCA). Because of the explosion of illegal immigration and the resulting arrests and deportations, in 1984 CCA got a federal contract to begin building and running holding camps for the Immigration and Naturalization Service (INS). And in 1992, the first private prison allowed to handle maximum-security prisoners was opened up in Leavenworth, Kansas. As of this writing, there are approximately 190 privately run prisons in this country that employ more than 10,000 corrections officers.

Of all law enforcement jobs, corrections is right at the bottom of the barrel as far as prestige goes. Corrections officers just can't get any respect. There are many reasons for this. For one thing, corrections officers are seldom allowed to carry guns except perhaps in the towers. Besides that, they are confined to the facility they work at instead of driving around in squad cars and getting in high-speed chases. There aren't any donut shops in prisons, either. I've seen surveys in which corrections officers themselves rate their jobs as crappy, and as a group, corrections officers report low self-esteem. Even G. Gordon Liddy hates them.

Another reason that corrections officers are sneered at is the way they have traditionally been portrayed in books, movies, and on television. I don't think I've ever seen a prison movie that showed the prison guards to be anything other than a bunch of corrupt, brutal, sadistic, perverted thugs. It reminds me of the way the media portrayed us Vietnam veterans when we came home.

So why do I rate this job so high on the private security hierarchy? One reason it's up there is that all corrections officers, whether working at private or state-run facilities, do pretty much the same work. Being a security guard is very different than being a street cop, but working in a private correctional institution is really no different than doing it in a federal joint. The pay is pretty good, too, compared with other private security jobs, and so are the benefit packages. Training is generally fairly thorough, and as I mentioned earlier, there is good job security and plenty of room for advancement.

After an offender is apprehended and brought to trial, the guilty son-of-a-bitch is pretty much forgotten once he or she goes into lockup to serve time. Also forgotten is the fact that these convicts must be fed, clothed, sheltered, medicated, exercised, entertained, educated, and guarded by corrections officers for the next 10 or 20 years. I see more and more information coming out that describes what corrections officers actually do on the job, and this is good.

I'll never forget my first day on the job as a federal "hack." Back then, in the early 1970s, the Federal Bureau of Prisons (FBP) was still hiring mostly veterans. They were assumed to already know a little about such matters as instilling and maintaining order and discipline, shooting guns, controlling rioters, and the like, so most of the training we got was on the job. I was assigned to an old hack who had been doing the work for about 20 years, and he was taking me around on a tour of the medium-security joint I'd been assigned to.

"So," I asked him, as we walked across the exercise yard, "just what exactly do we do here?"

"Ain't nothin' to it, Wade," he answered, after taking time to spit out a glob of chewing tobacco juice, "just don't let 'em fight, fuck, or escape!"

There's a little more to it than that, of course, but that sort of gives you the idea of the main duties of a corrections officer.

OVERVIEW

Most private prisons are minimum-security institutions or places such as holding camps or jails where people are locked up on a short-term basis. It appears, however, that more and more medium-security prisons, such as the women's correctional facility in New Mexico, are also being built and run by the private sector. The really rotten apples of society are in the maximum-security prisons, though, and except for one or two private facilities, most maximum-security joints are run and operated by the state and federal systems.

At minimum-security facilities, the inmates are under light supervision and usually are allowed to leave the grounds during the day for work or furlough. The prisoners are there either for nonviolent crimes or because they are near the end of long sentences for more serious offenses and are being "transitioned" back into society.

Many halfway houses are now run and managed by private enterprise, and there the security is even lighter. These halfway houses are located in the community, and the work there is about like being a dorm monitor in college. The "residents" are required to sign in and out, must be back in their rooms by a certain time at night, are routinely tested for drug abuse, and so on.

The tighter the security of a prison, the more work there is for corrections officers to do. Once you've locked a person in a cell, you've got to wait on that person. His meals have to be served to him; reading material, mail, and so on must be delivered; and every time you let the person out of his cage, special care must be taken, just as if you were dealing with a dangerous wild beast—which is exactly the case!

Corrections officers work under strict guidelines these days. Just about all activity is monitored and recorded on CCTV to be used as evidence in case of lawsuits filed by inmates or additional charges filed by the prison against an inmate. Although some charges of brutality and sexual assault leveled against corrections officers by inmates are actually legitimate, practically all violence and rape committed against inmates is done by other inmates. Protecting the convicts from each other is one of a corrections officer's main duties.

The other main duty of a corrections officer—that of not letting the prisoners escape—is a full-time job and a real challenge. Humans are clever animals, and when you lock them up and give them hours, days, and years to do nothing but scheme about how to get loose, some of them will pull it off. I specialized in prison security when I worked for the fed system, and enjoyed this part of the job much more than I did some of the other duties I had to perform.

These days, fewer and fewer young people are serving in the military, so police agencies and correctional facilities don't have the large pool of veterans to draw from any more. Kids are told that to be a cop or a prison hack they need to go to college and study sociology, psychology, penology, law enforcement science, public administration, and the like. Many of these kids, newly graduated from college and burning with the desire to use their newly acquired knowledge to help improve the "awful correctional system," end up in a cell block serving meals to the locked-up animals and wondering what the hell they got themselves into.

It is beyond the scope of this book to go into more detail about what corrections officers do on the job. Much has been written on the subject, and many books are available. If you are interested in being a corrections officer, whether in the private or public sector, I advise you to do some research first. Read not only the books put out by "the system" but also some of those written by current and ex-cons. The truth of what to expect on the job is found somewhere in between the two versions.

Like other cops, corrections officers don't open up much to outsiders when discussing their jobs—but if you can befriend a corrections officer and feed him or her a few drinks, you might get to hear some "interesting" stories. In the spirit of full disclosure, I have to tell you that I didn't care much for this line of work and only did it for five years. When I walked out the gate for the last time, I told the tower guard to shoot me if I ever came back to get rehired.

TRAINING

As is usually the case with the private sector in security work, the training provided to private corrections officers varies greatly. Because prison conditions are more closely monitored than other sectors of private security, you can expect some pretty fair training. In some states, corrections officers in the privately run prisons go through the same training academies as those in the public sector. You can expect classes on prison security and procedures, face-to-face communications, use of nondeadly force, hand-to-hand combat, riot control, use of baton and pepper sprays, proper use of restraints such as handcuffs and leg shackles, and possibly some training in firearms use.

PAY AND BENEFITS

Compared with other private security jobs, private corrections pays well. You will earn two to two and a half times what a regular unarmed security guard earns. That's the good part. The bad part is that ol' bottom line. Although you do the same work as a corrections officer in the public sector, you will earn substantially less for it than your county, state, or federal counterparts. Here are some figures I scrounged off the Internet:

- In 1998, the average wage for a federal corrections officer was $32,600 per year
- State corrections officers earned $27,300 and
- Corrections officers in the private sector averaged $18,500.

None of these wages are all that hot, especially since today's average income in the United States is about $35,000 per year. It's pretty hard to pay off your college loan earning this kind of chicken feed, and it's one of the reasons all prison systems are having so much trouble finding good people to do the work.

The health and life insurance benefits in private corrections are also better than average for the private security industry, but are not be as good as those for officers in the public sector. You are provided uniforms and equipment free of charge, however.

QUALIFICATIONS

The qualifications required of a corrections officer in the private sector are the same as those required to work in corrections for a government agency. You must be at least 18 years old, be either a U.S. citizen or have a resident alien work permit, be a high school graduate, have no prior felony convictions, and be sound in mind and body. Because so many high schools these days are not doing their jobs, you might have to pass a written test to determine whether you can read and write English and perform basic math. You may be given other written tests that determine your psychological qualifications, and you might also get to talk to a shrink. So regardless of what you see in the movies, if you are a sadist, sex pervert, or some other type of deviate, you need to look elsewhere for work.

Besides simply having no felony convictions, your background will be scrutinized for such things as evidence of drug or alcohol abuse, a tendency toward fighting and violence, and a bad credit history. There are two reasons your credit history is important. For one thing, it gives an indication of your general reliability and maturity. Perhaps more important, it gives an indication of how easily you might be tempted to take bribes to perform such illicit activities as smuggling in contraband, passing letters or notes to the outside world, or doing hundreds of other things that the inmates might dream up.

In some parts of the country, being bilingual in English and Spanish is a big help, especially if you are applying to work one of those INS holding camps. Your sex, race, and so forth are not supposed to be hiring factors, though in reality quotas are in place and so is prejudice.

Although the minimum age for corrections work is only 18, you will have a better chance of employment if you are older. From my personal experience in corrections, younger officers have a harder time of it with the inmates than older ones. I think the best age range for a corrections officer is between 25 and 50. There is no maximum age limit stipulated for most corrections work (the federal system being an exception), but keep in mind that the job can involve dealing with violent situations such as "cell extractions," breaking up fights, and riots. This work can be highly stressful, too, and people with heart conditions and the like should stay away from it.

As in other security work I've mentioned in this book, being big, strong, and ugly doesn't hurt. Being a veteran of one of the armed forces also helps, as does prior corrections experience with one of the government prisons or jails. A college degree of some sort will probably help you get hired, but if you learned what you were supposed to in high school, the things they taught you in college won't really help you much on the job. Ninety-nine point nine percent of the inmates you deal with won't have the education and background of a G. Gordon Liddy, so your knowledge of ancient Babylonian history, knowing how to speak Latin, or mastery of some other arcane subject will be wasted. Street smarts are much more valuable.

FINDING JOBS

Finding prison work these days is pretty damned easy. County and state departments of correction advertise heavily in the newspapers, and the job roster for the FBP is just about always open. Private prisons are always hurting for people, too, and the only thing that might make it more difficult to work in the private sector is that there are fewer private institutions. Also, they don't seem to advertise in the papers as much as the state and county do, but private and public employment agencies can help you here.

The two major players in the private corrections field are the previously mentioned CCA and Wackenhut Corporation. You might contact their corporate headquarters and find out whether there is a private institution someplace near you, or at some location you would like to move to. If you have a lot of previous corrections experience, especially at the supervisory level, they will be very interested in helping you.

If there is a private prison or other corrections institution in your immediate vicinity, call and make an appointment to go by in person and apply. It's a good idea to take all of your documentation, such as Social Security card, driver's license, armed services DD 214, and any letters or documents from previous employment with other correctional facilities you may have worked for. It's possible you may be given a screening interview on the spot, so look presentable.

If you want to save a trip, the strategy of mailing a résumé works well here because the private prison can use this as a screening tool. Make sure you put in the fact that you are at least a high school graduate and list your military, corrections, or police background. You might also mention that you have had no prior trouble with the law and that you welcome a credit check. If they call you for an interview, you are about 70 percent sure of being offered a job, probably on a probationary status until you are completely checked out.

JOB ADVANCEMENT POTENTIAL

The possibilities for job advancement in private corrections are very good, especially for those with corrections backgrounds in the public sector. The turnover in this field is high, so those who stick with it will eventually move up. Correctional facilities usually use a paramilitary rank structure similar to that of police forces: The rank and file are corrections officers; there might be the rank of sergeant for more senior experienced officers; the shift supervisors will probably be lieutenants; and the overall corrections officer supervisor is usually a captain. After this point in the chain of command, the bosses start wearing suits and ties, and they stay mainly in their air-conditioned offices.

THE GOOD POINTS

As mentioned earlier, compared with many other areas of private security work, the pay of private corrections officers is pretty good, as are the health and life benefits. There is usually paid time off as part of your benefits package, and due to the stressful nature of the work, this may be quite generous in contrast to other jobs. You receive better training than you would in most private security work, and uniforms and equipment are furnished.

Job security is very good in this sector, better than in most private security work. Unless you really screw up by breaking a major rule or regulation, or are simply a lousy, undependable, lazy bastard, you don't have to worry much about being fired. As we have seen, the corrections job field is booming and there are no recessions in crime and punishment.

The possibilities for advancement are also very good, and for those with a solid background in the public sector of corrections, advancement opportunities in private prisons are even better. If, for example, you have worked 10 or 12 years for a state prison and have reached the rank of sergeant, you might very well be able to find a job with a private prison as a lieutenant or captain. Private correctional institutions also hire many old hacks who have retired from work in the public corrections sector. A retired captain from a state or federal prison could very well go to work as a warden in a new, privately run joint.

Another reason a person might want to work in the public sector of corrections could be that the private prison is closer to his home than the state or county facility. Many correctionsofficers here in Tucson who work for the state prison make a 100+ mile round trip each day to the main institution in Florence. There is a privately run prison about 10 miles out of town where they could work instead.

You could probably begin working in the private sector sooner than in a public institution or jail. Often the state and county correctional departments only hire once or twice a year. The hiring process with these agencies is complicated, requiring prescreening, interviews, testing, and attendance at a corrections officer academy before you can start work. Getting on with the FBP usually takes even longer because you must go on a roster of qualified job applicants and may not be called for an interview for up to a year. Usually things in the private sector are quicker. In most locales, a temporary guard card is all you need to become a probationary correctional officer in a private institution.

THE BAD POINTS

The main bad point of private corrections work is that you can get a job doing the same thing in the public sector at a higher rate of pay, and usually with better benefits, too. There is also the prestige factor. Although there just ain't much prestige in this line of work no matter where you do it, corrections officers who work for the public sector tend to have an elitist attitude and believe that they are "real" corrections officers as opposed to the "rent-a-hacks" who work in private institutions and facilities.

Other bad points of the job are all those things that make the work disagreeable no matter whom you do it for. Corrections is scuzzy work, period. A popular saying among the hacks in the fed joint were I worked was, "This is the only job I know of where you have to wash your hands before you take a leak!" And this was in the days before AIDS and hepatitis C became a problem. You have to do a lot of shakedown inspections in a prison, and many times these are those much joked-about "body cavity searches," which aren't a whole lot of fun for the searcher or searchee.

The stress level of correctional work is high due to the constant confrontational situations. Most of the people regular cops deal with on a daily basis are normal, law-abiding citizens, but all the people corrections officers deal with daily are proven criminals. The inmates are on one side, and you are on another, and never the twain shall meet.

Corrections officers work in a different kind of world where everyone is divided into two groups. There are only the Strong or the Weak. This labeling goes for inmate and guard alike, and really has nothing to do with physical size or strength. If, for example, an inmate asks you to use your pen and you let him have it even though it is against a minor prison rule to do so, you will receive the label and reputation of being Weak, and may have to live with that for the rest of your term of employment.

Violence can, and will, break out at any time, and you must be prepared to shift immediately from a state of semi-boredom into action in the proverbial heartbeat, which is why people with cardiac disease should not do this work. As with some of the other jobs in private security, there is the real chance of serious injury or death. In corrections work there is the added possibility of being taken hostage during a riot or uprising and of being brutalized in numerous, unspeakable ways while the big shots hold televised negotiations with the convict leaders of the rebellion. If you get out alive, a visit to your proctologist will undoubtedly be in order.

A TYPICAL DAY ON THE JOB

I again offer two versions of what a typical day's work as a correctional officer in a private institution might be like. In the first scenario, you are a 30-year-old female officer working in a medium-security prison for male offenders. You have four years' corrections experience working in the federal prison system. In the second scenario you are a 50-year-old male who retired from a career with the state prison and is now working as a monitor for a privately run halfway house.

Example One

After you got out of high school, you served four years as a marine. After you got out, you went to junior college and got an associate degree in criminal justice. The FBP was recruiting heavily for female Spanish-speaking officers, and because you fit both categories you went right to work, not having to wait a year or two like most of the male applicants.

You discovered that you didn't mind prison work and were pretty good at it. At your height of 5 foot 10, and carrying a solid 180 pounds, you have never been what could be considered dainty and feminine. Growing up, you always preferred lifting weights and playing football with the boys to playing with dolls. Although you are not a lesbian, most of the male inmates think you are, and this makes things easier when dealing with them.

The only thing you didn't like about working for the FBP was the location of the prison you were assigned. You wanted to move back to the California where you were raised, and transferring with the FBP was difficult and took time. You got wind of a position with a new, private prison that had recently opened up in your hometown, and when you contacted it, you were assured a job if you left the federal system. So that's what you did.

The private prison where you now work is an all-male, medium-security facility. It employs both male and female officers. You are working the 3 P.M. to 11 P.M. shift in a 100-man, dormitory-style building. This building contains offices and an inmate dayroom in the center, and 50 rooms along corridors at each end. Two inmates occupy each room. This building is considered an "honor dorm," and to be assigned there the prisoners must have demonstrated good behavior.

When you report for duty this day, you first attend the shift briefing and are told that tensions are high in the prison. A big shipment of drugs has somehow been smuggled in, and the inmates all know it. There is bound to be trouble on the yard as the drugs are divided, sold, and distributed. Right now, there is a lot of tension between the blacks and the Hispanics, and it could bust loose at any time. After the briefing, you and your male partner draw your keys and relieve the day shift at the dorm.

At this prison, the corrections officers carry radios, body alarms, handcuffs, batons, and pepper spray on their belts. The prison is surrounded by a double row of chain-link fence with razor wire on top. There are no gun towers, but the electrified and alarmed fence is constantly monitored by CCTV camera. The inmates of your dorm are free within the prison from 7

A.M. to 7 P.M. They are allowed to attend classes, work in the prison industries building, talk to their counselors, or use the well-equipped gym. The prison is locked down at the 7 P.M. buzzer, and all inmates in your dorm must be standing at the doors to their rooms at that time for a head count.

An hour or so after you assume duty, you and your partner see a fight in progress right outside the door to your dorm. You immediately get on the radio and inform the control center of the situation. Two prisoners are going at it pretty good, but no weapons are in evidence. You and your partner wait for two other officers from the yard to arrive, then while your partner keeps an eye on things in the dorm, you step outside and help the yard officers break up the fight.

One of the men in the fight is a resident of your dorm. Since both men receive disciplinary reports (known as "shots") and are hauled off to be locked in segregation (the "hole"), the inmate from your building must be taken off the head count and his personal belongings inventoried, packed, and locked up to prevent pilferage by other inmates. Also, a full report must be written and filed. You finish all these chores just in time for the evening lock-up and count. The count is good, and you phone the number in to the control center.

Between 7 and 11 P.M. the inmates are allowed to roam freely in the dorm. Most go to the dayroom to watch television, and others play Ping-Pong, read, or visit each other in their rooms. All the inmate rooms must be left open during this period so that you can make sure there is nothing funny going on while you make your frequent rounds.

Not many of the inmates are watching television on this night, and most have requested to be locked in their rooms. When you make your check of the dayroom at 10 P.M., there are only a few inmates still there, and from the way they're acting you immediately know from experience that something is going on. You suspect either an escape plot or maybe something to do with the sale and distribution of the new drug shipment. You meet with your partner in the office, tell him your suspicions, and decide to try catch the culprits in the act.

The two of you are pretending to do paperwork in the office when a scout saunters past the door and casually glances in to check you out. As soon as the scout is gone, you slip quietly back to the door to the dayroom and burst in. There was something going on all right, but it wasn't an escape attempt or a drug deal. You catch one of the overt homosexuals, who goes by the name of "Monica," performing oral sex on one of the other inmates while a third watches.

The guy Monica is servicing sees you and immediately pulls loose. It makes a noise like pulling a cork from a bottle. All three guilty men stand looking at you silently, waiting to see your reaction. You have a choice, and you know it. You can simply pretend that you didn't see anything happening, and lock the three of them in their rooms for the night. This course of action would save you a lot of work and hassle. But all three inmates know that you know what was going on, and if you fail to enforce the rules against illicit sex, you will be labeled Weak, and from then on there will be blowjobs taking place in every dorm you work.

You tell them they are busted and escort them to the office. Each swears that they weren't doing anything wrong and that you are picking on them because they are white and you are Hispanic. You phone the control center and tell them that you have three to be transported to the "hole." Then, as your partner makes a final security round for the night, you begin writing the "shots," and inventorying the three men's personal belongings. Your relief shift arrives at 11 P.M., but it takes you an additional hour to finish what you started. There is a rule at this prison that the officer who writes the "shot" must personally do the paperwork, the inventory, and all the rest of it before getting off duty that shift.

You are tired when you finally get home, but know you did a good day's work and feel proud of yourself.

Example Two

You were only 50 years old when you retired from the state joint where you worked for 25 years, and you've decid-

ed to put in a few more years of work before you hit the rock-
ing chair on the porch. A friend from the department of corrections clued you in about a pud job that was getting ready
to open up at a halfway house right there in the city you live
in. In fact the job is only four blocks from your apartment.

The job didn't pay much, you discovered during your job
interview, but it was easy money and you beat out several other
applicants for the position. You are assigned to the day shift, and
work between 8 A.M. and 4 P.M.—real banker's hours. You wear
civilian clothes and carry no equipment or weapons.

On this day you relieve the night shift person, a woman,
about 10 minutes early as usual, and she tells you that things
are fairly normal with the exception that one of the residents
didn't return the previous night. She has already written the
report and phoned it in to the proper parole officer, so there
is nothing much for you to do but read the morning paper,
drink coffee, and eat your sweet roll.

There are a total of 10 residents at this facility, six men
and four women. They are required to get up on their own in
the morning, make their beds, and clean their rooms before
leaving for the day. Some of them have jobs, and some are
attending schools of different kinds. By 9:30 that morning, all
the residents have departed, signing out as required. You
make a round to check their rooms and do a quick shakedown in each for contraband. You find nothing illegal that
morning, but you see that one of your "problem children" has
failed to make her bed or empty her trash can. You return to
your office and write her up for it.

At about noon, the missing man from the night before
returns to the halfway house. He is hung over, dirty, and
shows signs of having been in a fight of some sort. The man
goes to his room, collapses on his bed, and zonks out. You call
the man's parole officer, who calls the city police, and about
half an hour later they come and take the poor bastard off to
jail. The parole officer calls you a couple of hours later and
lets you know that the man won't be returning because he is
headed back to prison.

By three in the afternoon, several residents have returned to the facility and signed back in. They hold a small A.A. meeting in the dayroom. At 10 minutes to four your relief arrives. He is another retired prison employee, and you retell each other a couple of prison stories before you pick up your lunch box and walk home for the evening.

It's a tough job, you like to tell people, but someone has to do it!

CONCLUSION

That's about it for private prison work. Although it is near the top of the scale for private security work, keep in mind that you can probably get a job doing the same sort of thing in the public sector and be better paid for it. As I've mentioned, however, there are such reasons as close location, advancement opportunities, or quickness of hire that may induce you to go with the private sector instead.

Although private corrections work involves little use of firearms, it can still be dangerous work. Next we will look at another dangerous job, one that does involve firearms, that of armed courier.

CHAPTER 6

Armed Courier

T o me, armored-car work is the quintessential example of what armed, uniformed, private security is all about. There are several reasons that this job is in the top three of the private security hierarchy, and one reason is that it is dangerous work. Many armored-car workers develop a nonchalant attitude toward the job after doing it for several months or years and seeing nothing but the same routine. "He always told me that it's not really dangerous work," is the usual quote you see in newspapers when friends and relatives of deceased armored car couriers are interviewed after a robbery. Guess what? Armored car work really *is* dangerous, and can get you killed, especially if you let your guard down.

Another reason this work is so high on the scale is the history. Hiring armed guards to transport money and valuables has been popular since money and valuables were invented. In the days of yore entire armies of paid retainers used to accompany caravans of loot and pillage, and in more recent times there was the horse-drawn coach with its strongbox and armed guard riding shotgun. As mentioned in the chapter on general armed security work, the mercenary aspect of hiring out to rich people to do work that they can't and won't do appeals to me for some reason.

The modern era of armed transport services began in 1859 when Washington Perry Brink started his company. Brink's is now the best known and established armed transport company in the world, with 160 branch operations in the United States, 40 in Canada, and 50 affiliates in other countries around the globe. "Brink's truck" is almost a generic term for armored transport vehicle.

Another reason that armored transport work is so high in the hierarchy is that you can count on not having your paycheck bounce. Besides Brink's, there are only a few other big players in the armed transport game, such as Loomis Fargo and Armored Transport. This is because it takes a large capital investment to get started in the armored-car business, and this keeps most of the fly-by-night, quick-buck artists out of the industry. Those "Brink's trucks" are not exactly cheap, and even the less expensive armored van costs as much or more than a luxury sedan.

OVERVIEW

There is a certain amount of prestige that goes with being an armed courier. Although people enjoy sneering at rent-a-cops, often making snide comments to them and so on, you don't see anyone in their right mind harassing armed couriers while they're on the job. Kill and rob them, yes; tease and make fun of them, no.

The pay and benefits in this job are about as good as you can get as a uniformed private guard. Like all the rest of private security work, the wages aren't exactly off the map, but they are higher than you will get elsewhere. The benefits are also quite good, with some interesting perks thrown in. One armored car outfit I know of offers a $10,000 reward to their couriers if they prevent an armed robbery, which in most cases means shooting and killing the robber.

There are some different types of job you might do as an employee of an armed transport company. Besides the most obvious high-profile work with armored cars, you might work as an ATM repairman, as an armed guard at the company terminal, or in the money room.

Working in the armored section is not only the most dangerous job, but also the hardest.

Money is heavy, especially when in coins. Armored cars run a daily route that might cover as many as 30 or 40 businesses. That's 30 or 40 times the courier has to get out of the truck, make his pickup, and climb back inside. Besides the weight of the money, he also carries the weight of his body armor, weapon, ammunition, and radio. Once back inside the truck on the way to the next stop, the courier doesn't get to relax much; there is accounting paperwork to do after each stop. The driver doesn't have it so easy either (although driving is usually considered easier than "jumping"), especially in cities with traffic problems. Although the modern armored car is air-conditioned, in really hot conditions the air-conditioners are never sufficient to keep things pleasant in the back of the truck.

Repairing ATMs is somewhat different than working on the trucks. Usually the ATM repairman works from his home and uses his own vehicle, being on call for a set number of hours each day. When a repair call comes in, the ATM technician must respond within a given time. The repairman is issued a gun, beeper, cell phone, and the tools to do the job. Sometimes ATM repairmen work in two-person teams and sometimes not, depending on the amount of security needed and how complicated the job is.

The job of terminal security guard is often given to older

armored-car workers who can no longer keep up a heavy pace. Terminal security people operate the control center, act as radio dispatchers for the armored cars, maintain access control of the facility, and do general security around the terminal building.

People working in the money room count and package money. This is primarily clerical, cashier work, and requires a great attention to detail. If the books don't balance at the end of the day, things can get pretty frantic around the place until the missing money is tracked down. We ain't talking pennies here, folks; the people in the money rooms are handling millions of dollars a day.

Everyone at a terminal building is armed at all times, including the bean counters, office personnel, and usually even the damned janitors. Security is very tight. Would-be robbers take note.

TRAINING

I recently went through the training that Brink's gives its new employees and was very favorably impressed. It was the best training I've ever received from a private security outfit. We were given several days of weapons training that included one entire day at the range. Brink's isn't stingy with their ammunition, either. We practiced with both sidearm and riot gun, and were required to pass a qualification course. The two Brink's weapons instructors were experienced, well qualified, and prepared. One of these men had previous experience as a police instructor and the other was a former Special Forces soldier who had survived an armed robbery attempt with Brink's.

I presume that other armored car companies offer similar training. As Bob Burns, another ex-Green Beret and experienced Brink's employee told me, "We used to always lose the damned gunfights with robbers, but since we upgraded the training, we are starting to win for a change!"

The preemployment training with Brink's lasts one week,

and besides the weapons training there are the usual briefings about the company, the pay and benefit packages, general security briefings that include threat recognition, and training with the armored trucks themselves.

For those going into ATM repair, there is additional training. This training is given both on the job and at central training centers run by the company. The field ATM repair people do mainly first- and second-level repair, but third-level work is sometimes also necessary.

PAY AND BENEFITS

Expect to be paid at the top of the scale for armed security work in your area. In Tucson, for example, armored car couriers earn about one third more than other armed guards. In my opinion this still isn't enough to cover the risks involved, the strenuous nature of the work, or the fact that only high-quality people can be hired for these jobs. Unfortunately, there is that ol' bottom line again, and I don't foresee any improvements in pay soon.

Uniforms and equipment are furnished free of charge, with the exception of body armor. Armored car companies do not require the wearing of Kevlar vests on the job, but they highly recommend them and will help pay for one. Brink's, for example, gets a discount from suppliers that it passes on to its employees and picks up half the remaining cost if you desire to purchase a vest through them. This seems fair to me: the employee gets to keep the vest if he or she leaves the company.

QUALIFICATIONS

The basic qualifications to work for an armored-car company are that you be at least 18, are a citizen or have a work permit, can pass a physical examination, be drug free, and have no felony convictions. If you are going to be working in the armored branch and driving company vehicles, then you must have a valid driver's license and a clean driving record. To drive some of the larger armored cars you must have a commercial license.

Armored-transport companies are quite selective and closely screen potential employees. You will be required to submit a detailed personal history that lists all residences and employment going back for about 10 years. Unlike some security companies, armored-car outfits actually run an investigation on you to verify what you told them. A spotty job record with long periods of unemployment will raise red flags, and the investigators will be curious to find out if you weren't actually in jail during those times you claimed to have been in a monastery. Armored-car companies are among the few in the private security industry that still make extensive use of the polygraph machine.

The reason for this close scrutiny is because, unfortunately, many armored-car robberies turn out to be "inside jobs" involving current or past employees. Besides verifying the material on your application, a usual question the polygraph operator asks is: "Do you have any hidden reason to seek employment with this company?" If you are planning to rob the place, the machine will start smoking, a siren will sound, and armed guards will appear to escort you off company premises. Perhaps this is a slight exaggeration, but you get the picture, I'm sure.

Armored-car companies especially like to recruit newly honorably discharged service men and women. Such people have already demonstrated that they are reliable, know how to wear a uniform, and have some knowledge of firearms. Two other reasons the armored car companies like these people are that their backgrounds are easy to verify and will almost always be squeaky-clean.

For the same reasons they like to hire veterans, companies in this industry also hire many people with backgrounds in police work. However, one informed source (who will remain unnamed) told me that he has never had much luck in hiring ex-cops, especially the retired ones. As I said, armored car work is strenuous. "They just won't work hard enough," is how my source put it. I'm only trying to be honest here, so please don't think I am picking on cops. When my own father was getting older and wanted to retire from police work, he told me that the only other job he'd been offered was with an armored-car outfit. When I asked him why he didn't go ahead and do it, he said, "Do you know how damned hot it gets in the back of those trucks?"

A background in locksmithing, especially in repairing safes, is handy if you want to be an ATM technician. Some knowledge of electronics and computers is also very helpful. I have found out from personal experience that being somewhat limber and having good eyesight and an ability to work in cramped locations is also a prerequisite for working on ATM machines.

To work in money rooms, you should have training and experience in such jobs as bank teller, cashier, or general accountant. Previous work in banks or casino money rooms is helpful. Although working at the terminal in the money room is not as dangerous as in armored cars, there is still some risk. One of the women tellers in training with me at Brink's quit after attending classes that vividly detailed several armed robberies during which employees were murdered.

FINDING JOBS

Armored-car companies don't like to advertise in the newspaper. Check with employment agencies first, both private and public, because the companies often use the agencies for prescreening purposes. If you are still on active duty with the military but are planning on reentering the civilian job market soon, check with the people in your unit who help with this transition. Often armored-car companies list their jobs with these offices before advertising the vacancies publicly.

Sending in résumés and making the rounds of armored-car companies asking about employment often doesn't work very

well with this industry. Armored-transport companies are in a
sort of catch-22 situation: even though they need good people,
anyone who comes in off the street anxious to work for them is
automatically suspected of having an ulterior motive. For this
reason, they like to hire people through personal recommendation, especially if the person doing the recommending is an old,
trusted employee. Having a personal recommendation from
someone like a judge, police chief, or other person prominent in
the community would also help you here. Yes, we are again
talking about the old-boy network.

JOB ADVANCEMENT POTENTIAL

The chance for advancement in the armored-car industry
is pretty good. Many branch managers started as armored-car
couriers. You will also need at least some college education in
business management to advance much higher up than lead
armored car guard. Retired military people do well in the
industry: I personally know of a retired air force sergeant
major who, due to his military training and background in
electronics, became the resident guru on ATM repair and rose
to an assistant manager's position in record time.

Unlike some parts of the private security industry, however, there isn't much turnover in personnel, so you might
have to work harder and wait longer to get ahead.

THE GOOD POINTS

One of the best parts of working for an armored-car company is that the industry as a whole is well established and
well thought of in the rest of the business community. As long
as we continue to use paper and coin currency, there will be
a need for this service. I find, as well, that most armored-car
branch offices are well run and managed and adequately
backed financially.

Due to the nature of the job, applicants are thoroughly
screened, so you will be working with other good people.

During my training with Brink's, a man was fired on the third day of class because he was consistently late. He was a nice guy, but all of us in the class agreed with the company's decision to let him go.

I have already mentioned other good points of this job, such as higher pay, good training, and added prestige. One of the things I also like about this work is that you do something that is obviously important and needed. Many security guard jobs are mostly public relations-type jobs that have little or nothing to do with actual security. Although armed couriers need to be pleasant when dealing with clients, there really is no need or time for a lot of interpersonal chit-chat and related B.S.

THE BAD POINTS

Some of what I list here as bad points might actually be considered good points to others. For example, as I have tried to emphasize, this is serious work and can be dangerous. Some of us actually like the job more because of this added bit of adventure. Others, such as married men with four or five young children to raise, might see it differently.

Also, as previously indicated, working as an armored-car courier is physically challenging. For older people or those with mobility problems, this is a minus. For others, especially younger workers who get bored easily, this is a plus because the time goes by faster and there is physical activity.

For those who repair ATMs, the situation is similar. Some will like working out of their homes and using their own vehicles, others will not like putting the miles on their cars. Some will like the unstructured nature of the work, others will hate being on call and begin to dread the sound of the beeper.

A big minus to this work that just about everyone hates being closely monitored and watched at all times to ensure honesty. This can lead to a real sense of paranoia but it's simply the nature of the beast, as they say, and is something that has to be gotten used to. Money does go missing at times, and even though it usually turns out to be due to clerical error, occasionally it does get stolen by employees. Having to submit to periodic polygraph testing is another fact of life in armored-car work.

A TYPICAL DAY ON THE JOB

I give two scenarios once again, one that describes a day in the life of an ATM repair person, and the other in the work day of an armored-car courier. To help emphasize the seriousness of this work, the scenario detailing the armored car courier's job is not about a typical day, but includes an armed robbery attempt.

Example One

You are a 29-year-old male with an associate degree in electronics. You have decided that you are more interested in becoming a policeman than working on computers, so you have enrolled in college again and are pursuing a degree in criminal justice. In the meantime, you have begun working as an ATM repair person for a major armed transport company.

You are on call three days a week, from 7 A.M. until 11 P.M. You are paid a set amount for each day, no matter how many calls you run. Some days you have very few calls, are able to work on your school homework, and feel that you are really getting over. At other times you are running all day, putting several hundred miles on your car, and cursing every time you have to fill up the gas tank. All things considered, though, the job is working out pretty well for your current lifestyle and needs.

On this particular day, you have had three quick calls early in the day. Your damned beeper went off at exactly 7 A.M., and two more times while you were on the way to the first call. You had to pull off the road at each of these other two times to call dispatch on the cell phone, acknowledge that you had received the calls, and give an

estimated time of arrival. All three repair calls that morning turn out to be minor problems that are easily repaired,
but they are all in different parts of the city, and it is noon
before you return home.

The beeper is quiet for the rest of the day, so you finish
your term paper on "The Social, Moral, and Legal Issues of
the Juvenile Justice System within the Minority Family Unit,"
kick back at your apartment's pool for a while, then take a
nap. At 10 P.M., the beeper still has not gone off. You phone
the other repairman on duty, and he says he has had no calls
at all that day, and is going to go to bed. You are just getting
ready to crawl under the covers yourself when your beeper
goes off.

It is 10 minutes until quitting time, but you are required
to run the call. It is at a convenience store in the worst part of
town. Usually you would ask the other repairman to meet
you there for added security, but you know he has gone to
bed and you don't want to wake the poor guy up. You are
cursing to yourself as you strap on your Kevlar vest, a piece
of equipment that you don't always wear, but this time figure
might come in handy.

The company has issued you a S&W Model 64 revolver, a
fine gun, but one that holds only six rounds and is slow to
reload. Although it is against company policy, you sometimes
carry your personal weapon, a Glock 19 with a high-capacity
magazine and two spares on your belt. In the part of town
you have to go at this time of night, you take the Glock. Your
ATM repairman uniform is a jumpsuit that you wear over
your street clothing.

By the time you get to the convenience store it is almost
midnight. Things are jumping as usual in the store parking
lot. Kids with shaved heads, jail tattoos, and baggy clothing
are sitting around their cars out in the lot, drinking beer and
listening to loud music. Things get a little bit quieter as they
watch you walk in the store. You are careful to carry your tool
bag in your left hand to leave the gun hand free.

The store clerk, a female, seems glad to see you and your

gun. She points to the broken ATM, and you go to work on it. You have it opened and are in the middle of troubleshooting the problem, when two of the gangstas come in the store. They are being cool, just hitting on the store clerk, and only occasionally glance your way. You make sure you keep the ATM machine between you and them anyway, and mentally decide which one of the two you will shoot first if things get out of hand.

The problem is soon fixed, you secure the machine, and call dispatch to close out the call. Dispatch tells you to have a nice night, and you make it to your car, and home without further incident.

Example Two

You are a 27-year-old male recently discharged from the U.S. Army after spending six years in Special Forces as a weapons man. The last two years of your enlistment were spent with the elite Delta Force. You have decided you would like to work for one of the alphabet agencies, probably the CIA, so are going to college to get a degree in political science. One month ago you started working for an armored-car company as a courier, and find that the job fits well with your school schedule. You start work at 6 A.M. and are off by 2:30 P.M. each afternoon. All your classes are in the evening, so there is no conflict.

Because of your background and the fact that you had no problem maxing the company's weapons qualification course, you have been assigned to one of the more dangerous routes. There have been several armored-car robberies and shootouts on this route in the past couple of years, and the company is having trouble finding people to work it. It doesn't seem any more dangerous than the stuff you did in the army, so you have no gripes about the assignment.

Due to the added threat on this route, the company is using two-man teams for each pickup. One man carries a 12-gauge riot gun. The courier carries the issued pistol, an S&W Model 4046 automatic, in his right hand and the money bag in the left. The driver, of course, stays in the truck. You are the money carrier of this team, and your shotgun guard is an older, retired cop you have come to know, like, and trust. The driver is an experienced employee who has survived one robbery attempt before and knows the ropes.

You have just made your next-to-last pickup for the day from a busy department store at a mall. You leave the store and walk to where the truck is parked. The shotgun guard faces out, holding the gun at port arms, while observing the lot. You holster your pistol to reach up and open the truck door. You've just swung the door open, when things go to hell.

The shotgun guard's head explodes, splattering you with brains and blood. Everything goes into slow motion for you at this point as the adrenaline surges and survival instincts kick in. The company training for this situation says that you should attempt to get in the truck for cover, but your partner is down and you don't know yet that he is mortally wounded. In a microsecond you make your decision. You throw the money bag into the truck, slam the door, and yell at the driver to get the hell out of there. You are aware that he is doing just that as you spin around, draw your weapon, and automatically drop into a kneeling position beside the body of your friend.

A man with a ski mask over his face is running toward you, yelling and firing a pistol at you. Your sense of hearing has completely shut down, so you are only aware of these things because his mouth is moving and you can observe the muzzle flash of his pistol. You notice that he is holding his gun in approved gangsta fashion, on the side, and at a level that is above his line of sight. Because things have gone into slow motion, you actually have time to be amused at how incompetent this robber is.

You also seem to have all the time in the world to bring your own pistol up in a two-handed Weaver, carefully aim at the center of your attacker's chest, and double tap him. He appears not to slow his rush, so you automatically follow with a third shot to his head. After this shot, your assailant falls face first on to the pavement about six feet in front of you.

You look around for more attackers and see none. There is no more gunfire directed your way, and you observe a Honda Civic departing the scene at high speed. The armored car is nowhere in sight, but you hear approaching sirens. Police officers and an ambulance are soon on the scene, and it is only then that you realize that your partner is dead and that you have been shot twice, once in the left arm and once in the center of your protective vest.

The investigation of the robbery reveals that the shotgun guard was killed by a rifle, probably an AK-47. He was hit twice, one round penetrating his vest near the neck, the other hitting him directly in the forehead. Your arm wound (which turns out to be minor), was also from the rifle, but the round that hit your vest was fired by the man in the ski mask.

After the autopsy on the dead bandit you find out that your shooting was very good. All three shots were lethal, one going through his heart, one passing through both the heart and the spine, and the third through the man's right eye and out the back of his head.

You aren't surprised at your marksmanship, because it seemed at the time that you were firing slowly and deliberately. According to one witness, however, your three shots came so close together that she thought you were using a machine gun.

The company gives you a $10,000 bonus, gives the driver $5,000, and pays a large settlement to the family of the killed guard, which includes a full college scholarship for his grandson. After you heal up, you go back to work with the armored branch, and other than having recurrent nightmares about the incident for the rest of your life, have no further problems.

CONCLUSION

Armored-car work is serious stuff and can get you shot. But because of this danger, the job has its rewards. If you are an active-duty military person who plans on leaving the service soon and think you might like to try some security work, you should look into the opportunities with armored-car companies.

The next chapter will explore the world of bodyguard and executive protection work.

CHAPTER 7

Bodyguard

"**B**ODYGUARDS WANTED! High pay, travel, adventure. Our three-week correspondence course qualifies you, teaches you everything you need to know, and guarantees you a pick of world-wide assignments! Send $500 in cash to P.O. Box 123." You have probably noticed this type of ad before. Perhaps you've even mailed in your money and taken what training was offered. Maybe you are still waiting for that list of job assignments.

Hey, being a bodyguard is way up there on the "cool scale," and this is one of the reasons it is so far up in the private-security hierarchy. Imagine being able to tell the chick next to you at the bar that you are a professional bodyguard. On the cool scale, bodyguarding is right up there with being a private investigator, a spy, or a mercenary soldier.

OVERVIEW

Let's try to get back down to Earth here. The job of bodyguard also goes by other titles these days, such as close personal protection, VIP protection, or executive protection.

Actually these terms often describe different job levels of the same field. When people hire a "bodyguard," they are usually looking for an individual, or a small team of individuals, who can shadow them, keep crazed fans at arm's length, keep jealous ex-lovers away, and beat up reporters or photographers who get too close.

VIP and executive protection usually refers to an entire security system of protective measures that includes not only the bodyguards themselves but such things as alarms, CCTV, security lighting, guard dogs, and "hardened" vehicles driven by specially trained drivers. Perhaps the most important thing these executive protection systems also do is provide either their own intelligence network to detect potential threats or to furnish a good link with government sources of intelligence.

It should be obvious that it is easier to break into this field as a mere bodyguard than as an "executive protection specialist." Down at the entry-level position there aren't too many qualifications needed to do the job. The work is similar to that of bouncer, which I covered in a previous chapter, and in fact many people who work as bouncers also do some bodyguard work. At the very lowest level, a bodyguard might be nothing more than a big, tough, ugly thug. He probably won't even be armed but simply depend on his muscle and scariness to keep people away from the client.

Moving on up the scale, you find people doing this work who are enthusiastic martial artists and/or shooters. These people usually have some training and credentials in both of those areas, and are legally authorized both to carry concealed weapons and to act as bodyguards in the jurisdiction where they work. Further qualifications might also include police or military experience and credentials from one of the better bodyguard schools.

Going another notch up on the scale are bodyguards who have all the above qualifications plus extensive experience in this field. This experience might be in the private sector only, or may include police work with any of the various units that protect local or state leaders and other VIPs. The gold standard for bodyguard experience is duty with the U.S. Secret Service.

The people who make it to the very top of the heap in this kind of work, the ones in charge of large, executive protection organizations, have all the above qualifications and have extensive leadership experience in the field. Items on their résumés might include: graduate of West Point, MBA from Harvard, retired Special Forces colonel, 10 years with State Department security, and so on and so forth.

I guess the point I'm trying to make is that simply attending a couple of shooting schools, earning a black belt in some martial art, and being a graduate of even the best bodyguard school will only get you started at the lower level of this job field.

There are many, many wannabes and phony bastards claiming to be personal security experts, executive security consultants, and the like. The actual experts in the industry hate this situation and have several organizations that attempt to sort out the qualified people from the fakes. The professional organizations, such as PSA Task Force, maintain databases of prospective bodyguards and personal security experts and attempt to authenticate claimed backgrounds, prior training, and experience. There is little control of the situation, though, and the fact remains that any yo-yo can hang out a shingle on the Internet as a personal protection specialist and start fishing for clients.

This field is actually larger and more inclusive than many people imagine. Besides those plainclothes bodyguards wearing dark glasses and earplug radio receivers, a large operation will include the aforementioned security chauffeurs. The VIP being protected also needs security at his residence, and this involves people monitoring the alarm systems and operating communications and control centers, and perhaps a high-profile uniformed security force with a couple of dog handlers thrown in. The intelligence branch of the protection team is particularly important if the client VIP is living in a foreign country.

Once again, there is a very mercenary aspect to this type of work. If you want to have steady employment as a bodyguard, you can't be real picky about who you guard. You shouldn't turn down a job offer from some billionaire rock star just because you don't like her latest CD—not if you want to eat regularly, that is. Of course this doesn't mean you should accept jobs working for known crime figures and the like. Criminals usually have their own people for security but this is something you have to be careful of if you want to stay in the good graces of law enforcement and keep out of jail yourself. There are many other legitimate rich people and businesses to work for.

A lot of this work is short-term, only lasting a few days or weeks. If you are lucky you might get a longer assignment with a large VIP protection operation. You will be working as a freelancer, mainly, spending much of your time nosing around for job leads. Many people who specialize in personal protection have an on-call arrangement with a private investigative or security company to do any bodyguard jobs the security company might require. Besides furnishing more job leads, by working for the larger licensed and bonded company, you will legally cover your own licensing requirements.

In all probability, especially when you are just starting out, you will need to supplement your earnings with other types of work. Doing part-time, generalized guard work for a contract security company or working for a temp agency are a couple of popular "day jobs" that can be dropped easily when, or if, you get that big bodyguarding contract.

If you work on your own as a freelance bodyguard, you will be expected to furnish all your own equipment. This equipment might include your weapon, bulletproof vest, and appropriate attire (which can get costly). Usually communications equipment is furnished, even if it is only a cell phone, but you should be prepared to handle this important aspect of the operation yourself if no one else does. The client usually furnishes any needed transportation, especially when he or she finds out that your own ride is a 1970 Pinto with one fender missing.

If you work for a large organization, most or all of your equipment needs will probably be furnished, especially if you work overseas. (Much of the equipment used in large security operations, such as the weapons, body armor, and communications gear are closely regulated in most foreign countries, so bringing in your own stuff probably won't be feasible anyway.)

TRAINING

Basically you shouldn't expect any training from the client. You were hired because you are supposed to already be an expert. The exception would be in a situation where you join a large VIP protection operation and need to be briefed on your role in the organization. This on-the-job training should only involve such things as telling you what shift you are working, basic rules of the game you work under, and so forth. If you are a phony who has managed to scam his way into the position, your lack of knowledge will soon be found out and you will be fired.

PAY AND BENEFITS

The pay and benefits of this type of work are highly variable, according to many factors. If, for example, you have a good reputation and a lot of previous experience working with Hollywood's elite, you can expect to make pretty good money. Rich celebrities in the entertainment industry are often very lavish with pay and tips for "the little people" who work for them. On the other hand, if you are working as a uniformed gate guard at some corporate estate, the pay will probably be right down there with what the local armed security guard makes. If you have lots of experience and have managed to work your way into a leadership position as head of corporate VIP protection, you can expect to be paid the equivalent of what executives in the corporation earn.

My advice to people just getting into this field of security is the same advice often given to freelance writers, artists, and actors: Don't quit your day job.

QUALIFICATIONS

The general prerequisites for being a bodyguard are the same as those required for the other types of security work already discussed in this book. You need to be able to pass any local licensing and bonding requirements, which means that you must be an adult, be a citizen or have a work permit, and be able to prove that you are of good moral character. You also need to be healthy and physically fit.

One of the main problems with VIP protection work is that there is no "controlling legal authority" in the industry dealing with certification. As I've said, anyone who wants to can become a bodyguard simply by assuming the title. What most employers look for in a personal protection specialist is verifiable training and a job history of actually doing this work. The best qualification is prior employment by any of several governmental agencies such as the Secret Service, State Department security, any of the alphabet agencies' security sections, U.S. Marine embassy duty, governor's protection unit of the State Police, or any work with local police agencies that involved VIP and dignitary protection duties.

In truth there is a lot of other good training available these days, and you don't have to spend 20 years with a government agency to get it. Several good books about the nuts and bolts of bodyguarding have been written and are available from publishers and mail-order outfits such as Paladin Press and Loompanics. The next step in your education should be to attend one of several schools for bodyguarding.

The bodyguard school I'm most familiar with and will use

as an example is Executive Security International (ESI). I have not attended this school personally, but do know people who have, and who are happy with the training they received. ESI has been in operation since 1980, so it is no fly-by-night outfit. It is also authorized to confer college-level degrees after completion of several of its courses. The training consists of a combination of independent home study and resident training at its facility in Aspen, Colorado. ESI claims to offer the most complete training of this type outside of the Secret Service or State Department, and I believe it.

As is the case with many other fields of employment, however, simply going to school and receiving a degree or certificate probably won't be enough to get you hired. You also need job experience in some area that is at least related to bodyguard work. This leads to that age-old question of job seekers everywhere: "If I can't get hired without job experience, how can I get a job to acquire the experience?"

FINDING JOBS

Because this type of work is near the top of the security job hierarchy, and because many people think it is interesting and way cool to be a bodyguard, there is a lot of competition for jobs. There is already a large number of people doing this work who have very impressive and verifiable credentials. There is an even larger group of people with adequate credentials trying to find such work. And, unfortunately, there are also those many wannabes and scam artists with no credentials at all who are competing for positions.

The bodyguard schools all claim that there is a lot of work available these days, and that is correct. What they don't mention is that there are many more would-be private bodyguards than available positions. ESI says in its advertising that it maintains an enrollment of 350 students around the world. Since it has been cranking out graduates since 1980, this means that this school alone has probably produced three or four thousand budding bodyguards. ESI and other legitimate bodyguard schools do not guarantee that they will find you a job after graduation, but they do offer a referral service, and this should be very helpful in your job search.

The truth is that just about all the really good personal protection job vacancies are filled through that prevalent network of old boys that I keep coming back to. One of the main side benefits of attending one of the bodyguard schools is that you will get a chance to meet and get to know other people in the industry who might be able to help you later. People with prior VIP protection experience with any of the aforementioned government agencies already have their own network, of course, and this puts them one up on those just starting out in the business.

Old-boy networking is used at all levels of bodyguard staffing, from the hiring of part-time freelancers to hiring for huge corporate security operations. Here are a couple of examples of how this system works.

First example: A visiting celebrity might hire VIP protection by contacting one of the major security companies in the area. If this company doesn't actually have any trained bodyguards on its staff, it will tap into the local network and provide the people needed for the short-term contract.

Second example. When a large corporation decides it needs VIP protection, it usually gives the requirements to its chief of corporate security. This person then uses his contacts in the network to locate and hire the most qualified person available to head the executive protection operation. This newly hired head of executive protection in turn uses his connections to locate and hire his staff, which might include specialists in intelligence, secure transportation, residence security, and personal bodyguards. Each one of these section heads are then responsible for finding and selecting their people.

It should be obvious that one of the most important qualifications each one of these various leaders has is his knowledge of the current labor pool of top-rated and available talent . . . in other words, their connections with the old-boy network.

If you are just trying to break into this field, your best bet is to associate yourself with a local detective agency or security company. You will have to take a few of the less desirable, lower paying jobs at first (what used to be known in the military as "ash-n-trash" jobs) while you build your reputation and résumé. Many beginning bodyguards are able to specialize by combining personal protection service with previous job experience in other areas. For example, you may already know something about communications security, or bomb disposal work, or have worked as a regular chauffeur. I know of a woman who was once employed in social services who now makes a living as a bodyguard working mainly with children and battered women.

JOB ADVANCEMENT POTENTIAL

There isn't much chance for advancement in this field. If you work as an independent contractor, you may eventually become known well enough to open your own agency. In the larger, corporate VIP protection operations, the people who end up with the better positions usually have years of previous experience doing the job either with the government or in the private sector. There aren't that many of these CEO positions available, so the people who manage to snag one tend to stay in the position to the bitter end.

You may attempt to improve your position by continuing your education in various aspects of the trade, attending different schools as you find time and money to do so. The more you know, the more chances will open up.

In my experience, however, most younger guys who try this work eventually drop out and find something less glamorous, such as regular police work or the military, which have defined, structured promotion systems.

THE GOOD POINTS

One of the best parts of bodyguard work is that it's possible to earn some pretty good money if you luck onto the right client. Many people get interested in this field after reading about the high pay, great perks, and good times one of those "bodyguards of the stars" is always bragging about. The "coolness factor" undoubtedly plays a part too, especially for younger men who want to do something different and exciting for a living. If you operate as an independent agent, you also get all the side benefits that go along with being your own boss, such as more freedom and a sense of controlling your own destiny.

THE BAD POINTS

I've read accounts written by Elvis Presley's bodyguards that say he was really fun to work for. Unfortunately, for every good client, there are 10 egotistical, lying, womanizing jerks that will want to use you as a pimp, janitor, and butler. There are stories about one famous male singer who used to have his bodyguards immobilize media people who irritated him so he could personally beat on them.

The work probably won't be very steady, especially when you are trying to get a start. You will have to worry about ensuring that you are meeting all the legal, licensing, and bonding requirements. Unless you are going into private bodyguarding from a similar job with a government agency, you will have to pay for your own training. You will eventually need to buy several pieces of rather expensive equipment, and have a wardrobe to fit many different occasions. Even though you hold a surety bond, a lawsuit can still wipe you out. There is very little job security with this type of work, even if you have landed one of those lucrative, corporate-security jobs.

A TYPICAL DAY ON THE JOB

In the following two scenarios, I give you a look at both ends of the spectrum. In the first scenario, you are a 25-

year-old male who is just starting out in the bodyguard trade. In the second scenario, you are at the top of the game—a 55-year-old veteran with the title of chief of VIP protection working for a large American concern operating in a foreign country.

Example One

You got interested in VIP protection when you were in the Marine Corps and assigned to embassy duty in Europe. After giving your four to the Corps, you got out, went home to the large city you were born in, and went to work for the state police. After two years you were bored and decided to try going into business for yourself as a bodyguard. You successfully completed training at one of the best private bodyguard schools, signed up with several private security companies doing on-call bodyguard work, and put your ad in the Yellow Pages.

Things have been pretty slow, but between the leads received from your old buddies on the police force, the occasional work that comes through the security companies, and your own initiative, you are actually paying your rent and eating regularly.

Your current job came by way of the security guard company, and you had to think long and hard before you decided to accept it. The client in this job is a visiting celebrity you have loathed from afar for years. You oppose everything she stands for, such as her shrill feminism, her pro–Viet Cong stance during the Vietnam War, her anti-gun activism, and her staunch defense of the former president. Still, she is rich, the contract is only for five days, and it pays more than any other job you have yet had.

Unfortunately the job has turned out to be even worse than you could have possibly imagined. This celebrity client has two young, adopted children who accompany her on all her travels. Your job, it turns out, is to guard these children between 2 and 7 P.M. That's only five hours of work a day, but it seems more like 50. You don't particularly care for kids anyway, and these two brats are the most spoiled, obnoxious little bastards you have ever had the misfortune of running across. The boy brat is seven and the girl brat is six.

It is your final day of this contract; you already have a splitting headache and are counting the minutes until it's all over. As usual, you have ridden in a chauffeur-driven car to the client's hotel and picked the two kids up from the nanny. As is the case each day, you are at the children's disposal and must accompany and guard them wherever they decide they want to go play during this outing. Today they want to go to Pizza Palace Kid's World so they can eat junk food and play the video machines.

The chauffeur, who sometimes sits with you for moral support, has decided this day to wait in the car. The Pizza Palace is jammed with other screaming children, the air-conditioner in the place seems to be malfunctioning, your headache is getting worse, and your Glock is gouging you under the suit coat that the client demanded you wear at all times. You glance at your watch and see that there is only about half an hour to go. There don't seem to be any suspicious characters hanging around the place, the kids are deeply enthralled by a game of Space Monsters, and you unintentionally start letting your mind wander.

Suddenly you snap out of the sexual fantasy you were having about what you and your girlfriend were going to do that weekend. Immediately you become aware that you no longer see your two charges. Your heart skips a beat. "Oh, shit!" you whisper.

Trying not to panic, you get up from the table and take a quick stroll around the place. No sign of the pair. Your heart is beating faster, and a light sweat has broken out on your forehead. "Stay calm, stay cool," you keep telling yourself. You casually check the men's room, but the boy isn't there. You ask an older girl to check the women's bathroom, and she returns with a negative reply.

"Are you looking for those two rich kids with all the tokens?" she asks you.

"Yes," you tell her, still trying to pretend that nothing is the matter. "Have you seen them in the last five minutes or so?"

"The last time I saw them," the girl tells you, "they were over there by the ice cream machine talking to some creepy-looking man."

Now you really are very near to panic. You know you should probably immediately call the police, but by doing so you will be admitting that you screwed up big time! Your pessimistic attitude has caused you to already expect the worse. You decide that you can write off any future you had in the bodyguard trade, and wonder whether you will even be able to get your old job back with the state police.

You make one more quick tour of the Pizza Palace, still don't find the children, and are just pulling out your cell phone to give the alarm when the two little creeps jump out from under a counter where they were hiding.

"Surprise!" they howl gleefully. "Fooled you, didn't we?" they scream between fits of laughter. "What's the matter, stupid," the boy brat simpers, "afraid we'd been KIDNAPPED or something?" More laughter.

You should be furious, but you are so relieved they are OK you simply smile and ask them if they are ready to go back to the hotel for the day. They say they are, and on the ride back they shoot spitballs at the chauffeur's head the whole way. Once the two monsters are finally delivered safely into the waiting arms of the nanny, you and the chauffeur go to the nearest bar and get ripped.

It takes six months to get paid for this job because the client's manager keeps "forgetting" to pay the security company. He only comes across after legal action is threatened.

Example Two

You went into the private sector as a specialist in executive protection after you retired from the CIA, and have been quite successful. You got your present job through an old friend, a retired general who had taken a high-paying position with the corporation after his long, successful military career.

You are heading a large personal protection department for an American oil company doing business in a Third World nation in Africa. You have been given free rein in picking your men and setting up the operation, and things have been going very well for you. All your staff people are men you have known and worked with before, and they are some of the best at their jobs.

Things have been relatively quiet since you got to the country two months ago, but since the intelligence briefing this morning, things have been picking up. Your intel officer, another ex-CIA operative, has several good sources with the U.S. embassy and the intelligence organization of the host nation. A new plot has been uncovered concerning terrorist threats against American businesses operating in the country; bombings and assassination attempts aimed at the business executives are expected to begin at once.

You immediately pass this information on to the CEO of the company, hold a strategy meeting with your staff, and set in motion your contingency plan for just such a possible state of affairs. A tactical operations center is quickly up and running in a room next door to your office, and a direct communications link with the embassy and the corporate home office in Houston is opened.

This is the kind of thing you live for and, as you sit at your desk scanning several incoming intelligence updates, you wonder whether you will ever get sick of it. According to the report you have just read, it appears that the opposition intends to attempt several ambushes of company employees when they depart for home that evening.

You call in your transportation officer and make sure he is aware of the situation. He assures you that the local military and police are working with him on the problem. All the drivers and bodyguards have been briefed and routes have been reconnoitered and secured as well as possible. Not only will the protected executives be riding in bullet-resistant limos, but they have all agreed to wear body armor this day for the ride home.

You double-check with your chief of residence security, and he tells you that all three of the company-owned villas have gone into a state of full alert. The uniformed guards, who are indigenous personnel, have been augmented by several Americans. They are all under the able command of "Wild Bill" Bradley, major, U.S. Army Special Forces (Ret.), who reports that morale is high.

The clock ticks toward quitting time, and you can think of nothing left undone. As the limos roll out the company gates, heading for the villas, you pop the top of an American beer, fire up a cigar, and stand by in the communications center to see what happens.

When, one by one, each car reports that it has closed station and there has been no attack, you are vaguely disappointed. "Oh well," you tell your communications chief, "tomorrow is another day."

CONCLUSION

There is a lot of stiff competition in the bodyguard game, but there are still jobs available for well-trained, experienced, and ambitious people. There isn't a lot of job security, and often the work isn't as exciting and glamorous as you thought it should be, but sometimes the pay, benefits, and excitement can make up for all of the shortcomings.

In the next chapter I will talk about the top job of the security hierarchy. That spot goes to a rather new type of security, one that doesn't even involve guns. It's time for "Revenge of the Nerds" when we get into the world of computer and communications security.

CHAPTER 8

Computer/ Information Security Specialist

F or those readers whose hobbies are shooting guns, going to the dojo, reading Mack Bolan novels, and leafing through Brigade Quartermaster catalogs, it is going to be disappointing to hear that the top job in private security these days goes to a pack of geeky computer nerds. Actually I am perpetuating a stereotype with that introduction, and had better add that many computer security people also enjoy those same hobbies that you gung-ho, kick-ass, physical types do. It's just that besides action-adventure novels, the cybersecurity people also enjoy reading magazines such as *NetworkWorld* and *eWeek,* and like nothing better than curling up with a book on some subject as cryptographic algorithms.

OVERVIEW

Before I start trying to justify my assertion that computer security is at the top of the security hierarchy, I suppose I should first explain what the hell "computer security" is. To be honest, although I have some experience with general communications security, I'm not much of an expert in computer security, so I had to do a little research on the subject. Therefore, some of the statements and claims I make in this chapter have notes, with citations. (If this style of writing makes your eyes glaze over, just ignore that part of it and *trust* me.)

The news media these days are full of stories about Internet viruses, worms, denial-of-service attacks, stolen credit card numbers, and so forth. This is only a small part of the story, however. The view that computer security's only purpose is to protect against outside intruders who break into systems to steal money and secrets, or simply for the fun of it, is not correct.

One book on the subject gives this definition: "Computer security protects your computer and everything associated with it—your building, your terminals and printers, your cabling, and your disks and tapes. Most importantly, computer security protects the information you've stored in your system. That's why computer security is often called information security."[1]

This same book goes on to say that there are three distinct aspects of computer security: secrecy (and confidentiality), accuracy, and availability.

Secrecy means that information is protected from being stolen by unauthorized people. In the case of the government, this might mean information on the latest neutron bomb or all those juicy secrets about the alien bodies stored at Area 51. For business, it means ensuring the privacy of such information as payroll data, internal memos, or proprietary business information. Two ways of keeping this information protected is through access-control measures and encryption.

Accuracy means that the system must not corrupt the information or allow unauthorized changes to it. These changes can be due to unintentional accidents, or due to The Phantom Cyberterrorist from Hell. In communications networks, there must also be some way of authenticating messages to ensure that the person sending the message is who you really think he is and that the sender is not under duress (picture a scene from a World War II movie where the captured resistance fighter is tapping out a message in Morse code to OSS headquarters . . . pan to the nasty SS man holding a Lüger to the radio operator's head).

Availability means that the computer system's hardware and software keeps working efficiently and that the system is able to recover quickly should things go to hell. The recent cases of denial-of-service attacks against some of the major e-commerce sites on the Internet demonstrate what happens when availability is degraded.

Basically, what computer security specialists do is to identify vulnerabilities and/or threats to the computer system, and then develop and employ countermeasures to protect against these dangers.

OK, is everyone with me so far? (Quit yawning, dammit!) Now that we are all on the same page, I'll tell you why computer security is currently at the top of the security hierarchy.

- It pays well. In fact, this is one of the few areas of private security work in which a person can earn a decent living wage.
- Tales of cybercriminals and cybersleuths are constantly in the news these days. Because of this media attention, and because computer security still involves rather esoteric knowledge, there is an aura of mystery attached to this job. Thus computer security has the highest prestige of any security work.
- There are no uniforms to wear, and much of the work can be done right from a computer security specialist's home computer terminal. Heck, when they are working from home, they don't have to wear clothes at all if they don't feel like it.
- The work is interesting, fun, exciting, and important. Knocking off a hacker in cyberspace can be just as rewarding as firing up a terrorist with your Uzi in real life.

There are other reasons I could give for this top ranking of computer security in the hierarchy, but if I've already convinced you, I don't need to say more. And if I haven't convinced you, then you have probably already quit reading this and gone out to lift weights or something.

Computer security people work alone, as freelancers, and as members of computer security companies. Some of their work includes doing security audits for private companies and government agencies, acting as information security advisors and consultants, and conducting penetration tests on networks to find holes in the security system. To me, one of the most interesting things computer security operatives do is to conduct a sort of cyberspace search-and-destroy mission to track down bad-guy hackers and give them a dose of their own medicine.[2]

TRAINING

Computer security people, especially independent operators, consultants, "hired guns," or whatever you call them are responsible for their own training. We all know how quickly things change and evolve in the computer world, so the security people must keep right on top of things. Unlike the skills involved in a job such as VIP protection, things that a computer security guru learned a year or two ago when he worked for some government agency such as the National Security Agency are now hopelessly out of date. People who are deeply into this business eat, sleep, and breathe technology, and constantly stay up on the latest whiz-bang techniques and gadgets.

PAY AND BENEFITS

You can expect to receive the highest pay in the security industry for this work. If you are working for a computer security company, you can also expect very good benefits. The rank-and-file computer security operator earns as much as most executives in other parts of the private security industry.

Computer security consulting outfits earn in the six-figure range for major security audits. A freelance, cyberhitman might pick up a grand or so for tracking down a cyber stalker and taking him off the 'net . . . and it might only take an hour or so to do it.

QUALIFICATIONS

One of the main qualifications for this work is simply having the desire to do it. The whole cyberscene reminds me very much of the Old West in that it was often hard to tell the good guys from the bad. There is a thin line that separates cops and robbers, and it is the same with computer security. Some so-called hackers or crackers get their kicks tearing stuff up, being bad, and generally playing the villain. People who go into computer security get their kicks playing against these cyberoutlaws. Many computer security operatives at one time worked the other side of the fence. Governments employ just as many people trained to attack in cyberspace as they do people to defend against these attacks.

The field of computer security is one in which what you know is more important than where or how you learned it. Degrees in computer science are nice in this business, but degrees don't carry as much weight as in other occupations. Just look at Bill Gates, the nondegree cyberhero of all time. In this fast-moving, fluid environment, half of everything you learned about computers last year in college is probably already obsolete.

Some training and prior work experience in general security operations or other aspects of communications security should help you. Many of the items on the checklist of a typical computer security audit are common for any security audit. (For example, checking for proper access control and documentation of access, storage of sensitive and classified material, whether or not employees are following the company's security policy.)

Some prerequisites for other security work, such as physical fitness, age, or health, are of no importance in computer security. Smarts count a lot in this type of security work, muscle doesn't.

There are specialties in the field of computer security, such as cryptography, that are usually learned while one is a member of the military or a government agency. Encryption is becoming more and more important in the business world, though, and much of the research aimed at developing new and better crypto systems takes place in the private sector, often in the math departments of universities. So being a mathematical genius isn't a bad thing to have on the ol' résumé either.

HOW TO FIND JOBS

The best place to find work in computer security is on the Internet. The second and third best places to find these jobs are also on the Internet. Computer geeks have their own old-boy network, and it's all in cyberspace. Most of the real pros in this game already know each other, so the best way to find a job is to join this in-crowd.

As in some other areas of security work, such as body-guarding, there are unfortunately many frauds and computer security wannabes—but the many knowledgeable people in this cybercommunity will quickly discover if you are for real or not and run you out of cybertown if you aren't. There is a lot of this work around for knowledgeable people, and once you build a good reputation you should have little trouble finding a job.

JOB ADVANCEMENT POTENTIAL

Things are very fluid in computer security, as they are in the rest of the information/technology (IT) industry. You can be a college dropout one day and a billionaire the next. Smart people with drive and creativity can make it big in this field, and do so with blinding speed. Unfortunately you can lose your ass just as quickly. Most people involved with the IT explosion enjoy this boomtown atmosphere, and accept the job uncertainty as a requirement to play the game. Many people who work with computers, whether in security or not, do so just because they like doing it; these people could give a rat's ass whether there's any advancement or not.

THE GOOD POINTS

I've already covered many of the good parts of doing this work in the beginning of the chapter. Of all those things I listed, the part that appeals to me the most is that you can do the job from your home much of the time. (I like the part about doing it in the nude, too.) Another good part of this job, which I failed to mention, is that there are few licensing or other bureaucratic hassles to go through to do the work. It's a very free atmosphere.

THE BAD POINTS

Except for having people think you are a geeky nerd, I can't really think of any bad points to working in computer/information security.

A TYPICAL DAY ON THE JOB

I have only one scenario for you in this chapter, but it pretty much covers all the bases. In this example, you are an unmarried 30-year-old college graduate with a degree in business who was spending so much of your time playing with your computer that you decided to do it professionally as a self-employed specialist in computer/information security.

Example

The lights of your bedroom come on, soft music plays, and the coffeepot has just finished its job. Your entire apartment is hooked into your PC and everything is fully automated. It's 4 A.M. and you have a big day ahead of you.

You get out of bed, yawn, and after stumbling through discarded pizza boxes and piles of dirty clothes, you make it to the bathroom. Some day, you mumble to yourself, you will figure out how to make the computer pick up after you. Sipping your first cup of coffee and still in your underwear, you sit down at your computer in your bedroom and go to work. You have three jobs to do this particular day, and two of them will be performed from your home terminal.

Your first job is running a penetration test of a client company's computer network. The company does a lot of business over the Internet and has recently overhauled its entire security system. You hum to yourself as you run through your little bag of tricks. You have little success with the more common attacks, but soon you spot a weakness in the system and are able to exploit it. Within two hours you have found three different means of penetrating the defenses. One of these attacks allows you to read the client's entire customer list, which includes each customer's name, address, and credit card number. After whipping out a quick report on your findings, you close down and take a shower. This job took only two and a half hours and earned you enough to pay your rent and utility bills for the month.

The second job of the day requires your getting dressed and leaving the apartment. You consider this a real drag, but since you have not been outdoors for three days, you figure the fresh air might do you good. Although you prefer working alone, you have signed on with a large computer security firm to do odd jobs for them. Today you will be part of their security auditing team that will work at a newly built aerospace contractor's headquarters. You dress for this occasion in your cleanest pair of khaki pants, your only white dress shirt, and your only necktie. You also put some new adhesive tape on your eyeglasses to hold the frame together.

The security company picks you up in a company van, and along with the rest of the team your arrive at the aerospace firm's gate at 10 A.M. This kind of work is boring for you because it involves little more than running down a checklist of items from the government's orange book. You are not really very expert at this type of generalized security audit but still uncover several flaws in the system, such as employees sharing their access control passwords with each other. By 2 P.M. you have finished your checklist and return to your apartment. Your pay for this four hours of work will be substantial because the security company does not sell its services for peanuts.

In the daylight your apartment looks even worse than you thought. The sink is full of dirty dishes, takeout food containers are scattered here and there, and the floor is littered with books, empty software packages, and old newspapers. To avoid having to think about cleaning up the rat's nest, you get on the Internet and play a few video games and chat with some of your friends.

You have one more job to do this day, and, because it's your favorite kind of work, you have been saving it for last. It seems that a friend of a friend's mother works for a large insurance company as a minor executive of some sort. A man she once dated has begun a campaign of cyberstalking and terrorism that is making the woman's life miserable. The authorities have been of little help, so you have agreed to do a little countercyberterrorism in her behalf. The woman is only able to pay you $2,000 for this service, but, since you enjoy this kind of stuff anyway, the money means little to you.

After a dinner of diet soda, a cold bologna sandwich, and a candy bar, you sit down at your bedroom computer and go to work. As you trace this cyberterrorist back to his lair, you find out that he is a worthy opponent and has covered his tracks well. At one point the trail disappears, but you are able to contact a person you know in England via the Internet who has even more experience than you at this sort of thing, and he gives you a new technique that soon has you back in the game.

An hour later you have the bastard where you want him! You have "taken him out," cyberally speaking, crashing the stalker's Web site, implanting numerous Trojan horses, malicious applets, and logic bombs, and ended the session by sending him a personal e-mail message telling him that unless he ceases and desists in his stalking campaign, you will continue with yours.

By 9 P.M. your workday is done, and since you have nothing on the schedule for the following day, you stay up all night playing Dungeons and Dragons with an opponent in Hong Kong.

CONCLUSION

In this chapter, I have tried to give you a brief look at what is currently the top job on the private security hierarchy of jobs. Computer geeks who read what I've written will undoubtedly spot the fact that I am not much of an expert at this stuff, but I hope I have been able to at least pass on the general nature of this work. And before the members of the techno crowd start making too much fun of me, I hope they will remember that not everyone in the world can be a nerd like them (only kidding, only kidding).

1.   Deborah Russell and G. T. Gangemi Sr., *Computer Security Basics* (New York: O'Reilly & Associates, 1992).
2.   Deborah Radcliff. "Hack Back," *Network World,* May 29, 2000, 52–54.

CHAPTER 9

Other Options

I n this final chapter, I want to cover a few miscellaneous topics such as managing a security guard company, starting your own security company, being a freelance security guard, and conducting overseas security work.

SECURITY MANAGEMENT

Down at the bottom of the private security hierarchy, working as an unarmed guard for a contract security company, it might look like the old boys who work in the office have it made. About the only time you see some of them is when you go in to pick up your paychecks, and they always look cool and professional in their dress shirts, suits, and ties. Heck, some of them even have secretaries. Looks to you like they work nine-to-five banker's hours, too. Each one of 'em probably earns $60,000 or $70,000 a year, right?

In the preceding chapters, I've tried to give an honest eval-
uation of career advancement opportunities for each type of
work. At the lower levels of the hierarchy, I said it was fairly
easy to move up into lower level management. With some
business education and maybe a little business experience, it's
actually pretty easy to become office manager of a large branch
office in a major city. The trouble is, things aren't as rosy up
there in the office as they might look from your perspective as
a gate guard at the manure-processing plant.

The office setups of security guard companies are all pretty much alike. At the bottom of the pile are paper pushers, or
the administrative section. This section is usually staffed with
women because that's who people expect to see shuffling
paper when they walk in an office. Depending on how big the
branch is, there might be from one to four people in the
administration section. There could be a receptionist/clerk, a
full-fledged administrative assistant, and possibly a human
resources manager. This administrative section handles all the
reams of paperwork necessary to document each employee,
and someone in the section probably also acts as supply officer to issue uniforms and equipment, accept deliveries, and so
forth. The work in the administrative section is pretty
straightforward and is similar to paperwork in any kind of
business. In the contract-guard industry, however, the high
turnover of personnel and number of part-time employees
makes it quite hectic. The people in this section earn about as
much money as an average guard does. The good part about
work in the administrative section is that it really is just a
nine-to-five proposition.

The payroll is a nightmare to keep straight in contract
security guard companies. The typical company might have
30 contracts spread out all over the city, each contract paying
guards at a different rate, and each contract calling for a different number of hours. Because security guards are notori-
ously flaky, sometimes not showing up at all, often coming in
late, occasionally working the wrong posts, it is very difficult
to keep track of their hours. Computers have helped things a

lot in this area, but getting out a correct payroll each pay period is still a full-time job. For this reason, some branch offices have a full-time payroll person or an entire staff of people.

Depending on the exact situation, the payroll manager might be the second-highest paid person in the office. The hours of this job are also supposedly banker's hours, but just before payday there might be a few 24-hour days necessary to keep things straight. The stress of this job is very high: workers complain swiftly, loudly, and constantly when their pay is screwed up!

Probably the worst job in the office is that of operations manager. This person is responsible for staffing the guard positions, interfacing with clients and guards to keep everyone happy, and trying to keep everything running smoothly. Staffing the guard positions means selecting the right person for each post, giving this person an initial briefing on what the post is like and where it is, and ensuring that a supervisor or other experienced person is on the post to train the new person when he gets there. Staffing also means being ultimately responsible for ensuring that a warm body of some sort is actually on duty when the contract calls for it.

The operations manager basically is on call 24 hours a day. Usually this manager is required to wear a pager at all times in case a crisis erupts. (Typical example: A guard hasn't shown up at his post and the manager of the client company is on-site screaming bloody murder and threatening to cancel the contract.) The operations manager must keep the guards happy or too many of them will quit. He must keep the clients happy, or they won't renew the contracts and the guard company will lose money. This job has high stress and frustration. It is a salaried position because if it paid by the hour, the operations manager would make more than the home office CEO. Burn-out rate is high for this position, and so is turnover.

The office manager usually doesn't have it too bad. He is insulated from contact with the guards and all the daily hassles, and his main job is usually to sell and write contract bids. If the guard company is part of a giant corporation, the office manager will be responsible to someone up there for bottom-line matters. If the company is not part of a larger organization, then the office manager might also be the owner. Office managers make good money, and work good hours, and the real superstars of the industry have plenty of job security.

Back when I was younger and had more ambition, I worked in security management for a while. I was a member of the American Society for Industrial Security, wore a suit to work, chain-smoked, and was stressed to the max. It was a salaried position, and the salary seemed pretty good until I sat down one day and figured out what I was earning per hour. It was something like 50 cents.

STARTING YOUR OWN COMPANY

It takes the average security guard about three days to figure out that the guard company is only paying him half of what the client company pays the guard company. Wheels start to turn, neurons start to fire, and before long the guard decides that it is more lucrative to own his own company than work for one. Some of these guards actually get their plans off the ground. They go through all the rigmarole to get a security company license, hustle up some financial backing (perhaps taking on a silent partner or two), rent office space and furniture, order a few guard uniforms, and, voilà, a new guard company is born.

Of course this new company owner has to find some clients, but that seems easy enough. All he to do is promise better service at a lower price and the world will flock to his door. The new owner submits his first bid for a large government contract only two days after opening his doors for business. His entire operation at the time of the bid consists only of the ex-guard, who is now owner and office manager, and his wife, who is everything else. A week after submitting the bid, he gets word that the contract is his. God, he's rich already and he's only been in business for a week! The contract is supposed to start in 10 days, when the old guard company pulls up stakes and leaves.

About this time, the new guard company owner remembers that the contract calls for 15 guards, and he still only has his wife on the payroll. He calls the local newspaper and finds out they can't run his first ad until the day after next. By the time his ad appears (15 High-Quality Guards Needed NOW!) there are only seven days left until D day. The day after his ad appears, only two people answer it. One of them is a street person who stinks so badly that his wife gets sick to her stomach and has to go home early, and the second applicant walks out when he discovers that this job only pays minimum wage (because the new owner underbid the job).

By the first day of the new contract, Mr. Owner and Office Manager has only been able to hire two people. With him and his wife also in uniform pulling guard shifts, they manage to cover the post for a few days, but then one of his new guards quits without notice, the other one demands a raise and a better shift, and his wife leaves him and files for a divorce.

A few months later we find our hero out of the security company business and back working as a fry cook where he wishes he'd stayed in the first place.

I'm not exaggerating much here, either.

BEING A FREELANCE GUARD

Another scheme that guards sometimes have better luck with is the idea of stealing the contract away from the guard company. The idea here is that if the guard company is getting $10 dollars an hour for the contract and the guard is only getting $5 of that, why shouldn't the guard cut out the middleman, work directly for the client for $8 an hour, and save everyone some money?

Occasionally this actually works out, especially if the client company is a small organization, such as a branch bank in a small town, and doesn't need much in the way of security. Back in the olden days, companies often hired the local retired cop, or disabled war vet to be night watchman. If you decide to try this route, remember that you may have to get yourself licensed and bonded as a one-man security guard company. You will have to buy yourself a uniform and other equipment. Also remember that someone will have to replace you if you get ill, want a vacation, or even a weekend off. The manager of the client company you approach with your proposition will probably think of these problems (that's why he's a manager) and decide to stay with the giant, international guard company already contracted with.

I've done a few short-term security jobs as a private operator, and things have worked out OK. Working in this manner is best if you know the person employing you well, or at least have a very good personal reference from someone who knows the employer. Keep the arrangement on the same level as you would if you were doing his yard work or hauling his trash. Ask to be paid in cash. Invent your own, quasi-official-looking uniform. Try to stay out of trouble and out of jail. If you do get in a jam, don't say you were acting on the advice of Leigh Wade, cause I ain't no steenking lawyer!

OVERSEAS WORK

Years ago, when I was a young paratrooper, there was a popular story floating around that if you got out of the army, you could immediately get a job in the Near East as a pipeline walker. This story had all the aspects of an Urban Legend in that it was unverifiable, always came from a friend of a friend, and sounded plausible enough to make you believe it might be true. The whole story was that after you were discharged, all you had to do was answer an ad in a newspaper, tell them you were an ex-paratrooper, and you would immediately be hired, furnished with a ticket to Saudi Arabia (or some other such place), and go to work as a security guard on an oil pipeline. You would patrol the pipeline on foot and would be paid some exorbitant salary for it. Sometimes the story had other embellishments, such as that if you killed someone messing with the pipe you would get a large cash bounty, or that every three months they would send you on all expenses paid, two-week R& R to the city of your choice.

Every few months or so this rumor would drift around the barracks. Remember Pfc. Smith who got out last month? I know a guy who dates his sister, and he told me Smith got one of those pipeline-walker jobs and is sending home $2,000 a month! (This was big money in those days, and Pfc. Smith was always some fuckup you would have expected to be in jail by that time, not getting rich.)

Most people who work private security have a vision similar to this one in the backs of their minds. In actual fact, even though there really are some overseas security jobs, they are hard to get, require excellent credentials, and require that you be a member in very good standing of the old-boy network to even find out about them. Ads in newspapers or magazines that read: "Earn big bucks overseas! Security personnel needed immediately. Send stamped, self-addressed envelope and $20 to find out more!" are con games.

I've run across some legitimate overseas security jobs, though. They are of two general types: Sometimes a large, foreign-based U.S. corporation employs a few security people for such things as VIP protection; these people fill supervisory, training, and management slots, and have extensive military, police, or government agency backgrounds. American businesses operating overseas do not hire security guards from the United States any more than they would hire their unskilled factory labor from the United States, pay their way to the foreign country, and then pay them huge salaries. That would be too costly.

Sometimes rich foreigners do hire highly qualified Americans to work in their countries for VIP protection, and/or as cadre and trainers for their own security forces. These jobs, too, go only to highly qualified and connected individuals. Although I'm now old, over the hill, and pretty much out of the loop, just a couple of years ago I got a query letter that outlined such a proposal. I knew this was legitimate because I personally knew and trusted the person it came from. The deal was that there was an unnamed, filthy-rich family in Saudi Arabia preparing to establish its own personal protection outfit and staff it with ex-U.S. Special Forces people. The pay for this two-year contract was quite good, and would be deposited in the bank account of your choice. There were paid R&Rs, and once a year there would be a two-week paid vacation to the country of choice. I sent in my résumé and never heard more about it, which is just as well, seeing that I'm a single parent with a son to raise, and for all I know the filthy-rich family might have had the surname of bin Laden.

The biggest trouble with those security jobs for foreign nationals is that they may actually turn out to be more like mercenary military work. If you do stumble onto something like this, you must be very careful to ensure that you will actually get paid and that you have a secure means out of the country if things go to hell. Currently there are some interesting jobs available in Latin America. But this work would be extremely dangerous, both in a physical and legal sense. If you go down there for one of these jobs, my advice is that you have your life insurance paid up and have a good lawyer on retainer. You'll also need to be fluent in Spanish.

Conclusion

The future of private security is very bright indeed. Besides the traditional role of private security as a guard of wealthy people, businesses, and money, the war on terrorism has focused a light on the private security forces used to guard airports, transportation terminals, government facilities, and defense plants. The infrastructure of the United States is an environment rich in targets for terrorists, and guarding it properly will take more resources than those currently available from military, National Guard, and regular police agencies.

I suspect that in the near future there will be many new job opportunities, many of them paid, supervised, and managed by the federal government. The American people now seem to recognize the importance of the role security programs and security officers play in stabilizing everyday life. Maybe after all these years, we in the industry will finally see an increase in pay and benefits along with better training and supervision. We can only hope.